BELLA

THE HARVESTERS Series also includes:

The Three Companions -
Pigs May Fly
The Land of the Palm Trees
Photo Finish

The Secret of Lilleshall Abbey

First printed October 1994
Reprinted July 1996

ISBN 1 872547 96 6

Published by Sherbourne Publications
Sweeney Mountain, Oswestry,
Shropshire SY10 9EX, UK
Tel: 01691 - 657853

Typeset and Printed by Clarkeprint Limited
Waveney House, Stour Street,
Birmingham B18 7AJ

BELLA

by

PATRICIA KNAPTON

Illustrated by Terry Walsh

Sherbourne Publications

TRIBUTE TO BELLA

This book is dedicated to the memory of a guide dog called Bella, whose love and devotion to her blind owner, Mr Charles Jackson, inspired the story.

'Bella' is based on her character, with threads of some of the events in her life interwoven in this fictional story. It highlights the duo's fifty mile charity walk in 1981 which did, in fact, take place from Wallasey in Cheshire to Bolton in Lancashire. It also highlights the danger of fireworks – which led to Bella's disappearance in 1984.

Bella was one of the many guide dogs who do a wonderful job in guiding the blind and visually impaired, giving them the freedom and independence to enjoy life to the full, and through this book it is hoped that her memory will live on as a very special guide dog and continue to inspire the public to support the Guide Dogs for the Blind Association.

N.B. With the exception of Bella, all characters and place names in this book are fictional.

CONTENTS

CHAPTER ONE: A FRIEND FOR LIFE

Bella nudged a cold, wet, nose into Tom's neck - it never failed. She had quickly learnt that this was by far the most effective way of waking her owner in the mornings.

"Hey, Bella," Tom said sleepily, "that tickles."

The intelligent black Labrador stood beside Tom's bed and watched him rub his eyes and then stretch, before reaching for his Braille watch on the bedside cabinet.

"It can't be eight o'clock already," he said, still half asleep, but his sensitive fingers probed his watch and confirmed that it was indeed eight o'clock.

"Bella," he said lovingly, "you are better than any alarm clock." Bella gave a swish of her happy tail before watching Tom snuggle back down under the bedclothes. "Just give me another five minutes, Bella," he pleaded.

Obedient, as ever, Bella obeyed without question. She sat patiently beside her owner's bed, listening to his rhythmic breathing. As a trained guide dog, in harness and working with her owner, Bella behaved impeccably. However, this was one guide dog with a mind of her own. She decided Tom had had his five minutes and he was abruptly woken again with a nudge.

"What is it, Bella?" Tom enquired sleepily. He put a hand out to stroke her and felt not one, but both of his slippers dangling from her soft mouth. "Are you trying to tell me something?" asked Tom, trying to hold back his laughter. Bella wagged her tail excitedly and dropped the slippers onto the bed.

"All right," said Tom, "I'll get up in a minute." However, Bella wasn't going to give him the chance to fall back to sleep again. She knew he had sensitive ear lobes and nibbled the one visible above the bedclothes, and it worked.

When Tom had finished laughing and rubbing Bella's ears playfully, he was surprised to feel something else in her mouth. This time it was his jacket. She had taken it from the back of the bedroom chair and felt so proud of herself as she dropped it gently onto the bed.

"My goodness," said Tom, still laughing, "you are an eager beaver this morning, aren't you?"

Bella stood panting and waving her tail happily with an added excitement Tom couldn't quite make out. He sat up in bed and wondered for a minute if he had forgotten anything planned for today but, no, he couldn't think of anything. Then it dawned on him - it was Wednesday morning and he smiled knowingly in her direction.

"No wonder you are eager this morning," he said, "you know the children will be in the park for their games, don't you?" The black Labrador wagged her tail vigorously.

Tom never ceased to be amazed at the intelligence of his guide dog. "I swear she knows what day of the week it is," he said, smiling at the thought. As Tom got out of bed Bella gently picked up his jacket from the bed and bounded excitedly across the bedroom and stood waiting anxiously by the open door.

"Just a minute young lady," he teased, "you don't mind if I have a wash and a shave first, do you?"

* * * * *

Outside the warm April sun rose over the small town of Seaton to kiss the day 'good morning', and life smiled. Spring was in full bloom and Tom's senses were alert to all its pleasures.

Bella, in her white harness, guided Tom as she had done for over seven years. Tom was a spritely fifty year old but, like his guide dog, he was young at heart. They were a great team, there was no doubt about that.

The morning sun burst through the gates of Victoria Park and filtered through the avenue of cherry trees lining the tarmac path that ran through the centre of the park. Tom may not have been able to see the picturesque cherry trees laden with delicate pink blossom and looking like Victorian lace umbrellas, but all his other senses were finely tuned to this beautiful spring morning. He lifted his head and breathed deeply, inhaling the perfumed air. "It's good to be alive," he thought gratefully.

Bella guided Tom towards the Dell which was ablaze with colour, as it was every year. It was a flowered haven in the centre of the park, with perimeter hedging for protection. Row upon row of golden daffodils stood to attention like soldiers with their trumpets pointing skyward. It seemed, as if by magic, the daffodils were playing the lilting music Tom could hear as Bella guided him down the crazy paving steps leading into the Dell. Bella pricked up her ears. Tom felt a slight pause on the harness and he knew that Bella could hear it too.

"It sounds as if they have the brass band out for us this morning, Bella, doesn't it?" He felt her happy tail wagging beside him as they walked past rows of tulips, crocuses and wallflowers, their scent was one of Tom's favourites.

Just then, Tom remembered there was a park bench about halfway along the walk. "Where's the seat, Bella? Good girl, find the seat for me." After walking a few yards Bella guided Tom up a step. He put out his hand and felt the edge of the wooden seat. "That's it. Good girl, Bella! Good girl!" He sat down slowly breathing in the scents of the gardens and listening to the sounds of the birds in the bushes, while Bella settled herself at his feet.

"Oh Bella, this is wonderful!" Tom sat back enjoying the tranquillity of the place that was his alone for a while, and he turned his face to the sunshine, surrendering to the warmth of its caress. Memories came flooding back as he identified the scents and sounds around him, no one could take away his memories.

Tom reasoned that he had been fortunate to have had his sight until the age of thirty-five. Then an accident resulting in a bump on the head, had robbed him of the one thing that he had always taken for granted, as most of us do, the use of his eyes. He had suddenly gone blind and from that moment on his life changed dramatically.

He had always been very independent, running a small but successful shop in the High Street but, of course, he had to give this up and found it very difficult coming to terms with the loss of his sight. He was given a white stick which he strongly resented and spent a couple of very unhappy years feeling sorry for himself and angry with the world in general.

Then someone suggested that he should apply for a guide dog. Eventually he did and teamed up with Bella. Once again his whole life changed, but this time for the better. A whole new world opened up before him, bringing him more happiness than he ever dreamed was possible.

Tom sat on the seat savouring his peaceful surroundings. The sound of bees humming from one flower to another and the birds singing happily in their chosen trees, was pure music to Tom's ears and, like the church bells he could hear ringing faintly in the distance, he felt completely in tune with the world about him. "This is the nearest thing to heaven," he told himself.

Bella suddenly turned her head resting her chin on his knee. His hand reached down to stroke her lovingly. We won't be long, Bella. You'll soon be able to see the children. Bella's tail swished the ground and Tom knew she'd understood. After all they only had to cross the remainder of the Dell and take the step that led onto the playing field in the park.

The sound of music reached the ears of walkers and joggers alike. Those with time on their hands stopped to watch the Maypole dance that the children from Seaton High School were practising; the music was coming from a portable cassette player. The dancers holding the red ribbons wove in and out of those holding the blue ribbons, making pretty patterns around the tall white pole below its garland of red and blue roses. Set against the green grass and blue sky it was a very colourful sight indeed.

"Come on!" shouted Mr Mason, their teacher "Keep those ribbons up, it's supposed to look like a gypsy's tent not a bivouac. No! No! No!" he yelled. "Stop the music!" He went over to the twelve dancers and tried to explain, yet again, that when he said 'reverse the sequence' he merely meant stop, turn and proceed with the same steps in an anti-clockwise direction.

"All right! Let's try it one more time." He signalled to the boy in charge of the music and the dancing commenced again. Mr Mason and the rest of the class, who were mainly boys because the girls were dancing, clapped in time with the music. A couple of boys sniggered as two of the girls almost collided with each other, but Mr Mason was not amused. The girls tried hard to get it right and finally the music stopped.

"All right, that's better," said Mr Mason. "With a little more practice we might make dancers out of you yet." The onlookers began to disperse and the games teacher called the children into a group.

"I want you to listen carefully to what I'm about to say." He paused for complete silence before continuing. "If, and only if," he emphasised.... "If you have the Maypole dance perfect by next Saturday, and by that I mean no mistakes, I might consider taking you to Barrington for the day. Tell me, how many of you know it is the Golden Jubilee year for the Guide Dogs for the Blind Association?" He was pleased to see a good number of hands in the air, although there were a few raised shoulders as well.

"Good! And, of course, you all know Tom and his guide dog, Bella, don't you?" This time all their hands shot up in the air. "Well, together they are going to attempt a sponsored walk of fifty miles to mark this special occasion and, of course, hopefully they'll raise a great deal of money for the Guide Dog charity. They will be starting off from Cheadlehulme where the very first guide dog was trained in 1931, and finishing at Barrington. Tom hopes to do it in five days. Fifty miles is a mile for each year the Guide Dog for the Blind Association has been in existence. If all goes according to plan Tom and Bella will arrive in Barrington on Saturday afternoon."

"Will the television cameras be there, Sir?" Jimmy Lucas asked, excited at the prospect of seeing himself on the Six O'clock News waving to his mum.

"Yes," sighed Mr Mason, "I imagine they will be, along with the rest of the news media. I'm sure it will be exciting, after all it would be quite an achievement for anyone to walk fifty miles, let alone a blind man and his guide dog." He smiled as he looked in the direction of some of the boys. "I know only too well the trouble some of you have, just walking to and from school."

A little voice with a big impact answered, "Not me, Sir, I go by bus." The rest of the class burst into laughter.

"Oh very clever McCreadie, very clever." Mr Mason waited until the laughter subsided and he had their attention again.

"If... If I may be permitted to continue... Thank you! Now where was I? Unfortunately, the seats on the coach are going to be limited. I'm hoping to take along a few teachers and representatives from school and, of course, the Maypole dancers. That should leave about seven seats to spare. Hands up those of you who would like to go." Almost all of them put up a hand.

"Not you dancers," he sounded slightly irritated, "you're going anyway. Now, let me see, can we have Jimmy Lucas, Claire Jeffries," and he reeled off names for the remaining five seats.

Looking at his watch, he said, "You can all have fifteen minutes to yourselves before we go back to school." There was a mad rush towards the games bag holding the footballs and other ball game equipment.

"Hey! Look! It's Tom and Bella!" someone shouted. There was a chorus of "It's Bella!" and the footballs were temporarily forgotten as the children raced across the playing field.

Bella had guided Tom to the bench they usually occupied at one end of the playing field. "Who's this, coming to see you?" Tom smiled knowing that Bella's tail was going at full speed, like a windscreen wiper in a snow storm.

"Hello! Tom," said David as he sat down beside Tom on the seat.

"Why, hello David, how are you?" Tom recognised David's voice from his many visits to the school where David was always the one delegated to see Tom and Bella safely through the swing doors, across the playground and out through the school gates. He had been singled out from the rest of the class for his caring nature.

"I'm fine thanks," replied David. He rubbed Bella's coat playfully as he continued. "We've been told we have a seat on the coach going to Barrington, so we will be there to cheer for you."

"That's champion, David. What about your friend Jimmy, will he be going with you?"

"You bet I am, Tom." Tom jumped momentarily, he hadn't realised that Jimmy was behind him with Claire and Rosie.

"Oh hello, Jimmy, I hadn't realised you were there."

"Sorry, Tom," said Jimmy apologetically.

Bella thought this was the signal for more play and tried to drag her lead around the back of the seat. Rosie and Claire made a fuss of her again. Bella could never have too much love and affection, she thrived on it.

As always, Bella was on the look out for a bit of fun and began to push her nose feverishly first into David's tracksuit pocket and then into Jimmy's in search of a ball. This not only tickled their legs but tickled their sense of humour and shrieks of laughter could be heard echoing across the park.

"I haven't got a ball, Bella," laughed a near hysterical Jimmy. But the playful Bella was not giving up so easily and she went to each of the other children in turn.

Tom sat enjoying the fun and laughed heartily along with the children. Blindness may have robbed him of his sight but not his sense of humour and his laughter lines wrinkled the skin at the outer edges of his dark glasses.

David went on to explain, "Mr Mason chose Jimmy, Claire and myself." He paused a moment, a frown on his face. "You know my twin sister Claire, don't you Tom?"

Claire reached for Tom's hand. "Hello! Tom," she said softly.

"Hello! Claire, love. Of course we know each other, don't we?" Tom said with a smile.

David went on, "As I was saying, Tom, there were only seven spare seats, we were chosen along with Basher, little Tim McCreadie, Melanie Brooks and Rosie here."

David paused again, he wasn't sure if Tom had met Rosie before. "Have you met Rosie, Tom?"

Tom looked thoughtful for a moment. "No, I don't believe I have."

Rosie wanted to be a model, she was very beautiful and David watched her intently as she shook the blind man's hand. "Hello! Tom. Bella seems to be getting excited about it all, doesn't she?" said Rosie as she let go of Tom' s hand.

"Bella's always excited when she's surrounded by children," said Tom patting his black Labrador's head.

Jimmy, still standing behind Tom, leaned forward and whispered in Tom's ear, "Don't say I told you, Tom, but Rosie is David's girlfriend."

David was over the seat in a flash, giving Jimmy a playful armlock. Tom quickly controlled Bella with one hand and raised the other in the air as if to act as referee.

"It's all right, Jimmy," he promised, "I won't say a word."

Rosie blushed as she heard David hiss in Jimmy's ear, "Even if it is true, you don't have to go around telling people."

Claire tickled Bella under her chin and the guide dog lifted her head as if she was asking for more of the same treatment. "I saw your photograph in the paper last week, Bella," said Claire, talking to the dog as if she understood every word. "You're getting to be quite a star, aren't you?"

Tom smiled as he answered for Bella. "Yes!" he said, "she certainly is and the newspaper people will be taking lots more photographs of her next week." Tom beamed a smile as bright as the morning sunshine, he was proud of her too.

"What is it like being a celebrity, Tom?" asked Jimmy now sitting on the seat beside him.

Tom laughed kindly and tried to explain to Jimmy. "Bella is the real celebrity," he said, "already she has raised thousands of pounds for the Guide Dogs for the Blind Association. Also, he added, "she has met many famous people, including Royalty." The children were really impressed as Tom continued. "She's had her picture in lots of magazines, some have even gone abroad."

Tom stroked his famous guide dog lovingly as he went on to tell the children about the scrapbooks full of photographs and press cuttings that he had at home.

An inquisitive Jimmy asked, "How do you manage.... I mean, to put them into the scrapbooks?"

Tom reassured him that he had a friend who visited him regularly, and she helped him. This merely prompted Jimmy to enquire further, "How do you manage living on your own, Tom?"

The friendly blind man was used to answering such questions. "Oh we manage all right, don't we Bella?" The Labrador wagged her tail as if to say 'of course we do'. "And besides," added Tom, "I have a very good neighbour who pops in frequently to see if there is anything I need."

Claire was fascinated, "Didn't you ever get married, Tom?" Tom smiled, and Claire watched his face light up as he remembered someone he would never again see.

"No, love," he said resignedly, "I never did." Tom admired the frankness of children, they asked direct questions, unhampered by the sensitivities of his obvious handicap and he felt comfortable with them. "Mind you," and he smiled at the memory, "I was very nearly engaged once." His smile vanished for a moment as a rather painful picture filled his memory, "But then I went blind..and she married someone else."

Claire felt a surge of compassion for this remarkable blind man and she reached out to squeeze his hand, a gesture that needed no explanation. She was only ten years old but so wise for her age. She also had some of David's caring qualities, "But you have Bella now," she said softly.

"Yes," said Tom, smiling happily again, "Bella is the only girl in my life now, and she's the best friend I'll ever have." Bella looked up knowingly as he stroked her thoughtfully, "besides she keeps me busy with all the charity work."

David joined the children as they sat around Tom, fascinated. David asked with an element of curiosity, "What happens to all the money, Tom. I mean.... who gets it all?"

"I'm glad you asked me that," said a much more bubbly Tom, as he warmed to his favourite subject. Nothing gave him greater pleasure than to extol the virtues of the Guide Dogs for the Blind Association.

"Well now..." he explained, "it all goes towards the cost of training guide dogs for the work they do. It costs a great deal of money," he stressed, "to breed and train the dogs at the many centres throughout the country, so we have to raise as much money as we can."

Tom turned towards David, "If my memory serves me well, you were away from school when I gave my talk about the Association."

David flicked his fingers, "That's right," he said as he realised, "I had flu at the time. I was sorry to have missed it."

Tom reassured him. "On my next visit I will cover all aspects of fundraising. It would take me more time than you have at the moment." David agreed that it would and Tom added finally, "I only know how much Bella has changed my life, she has given me freedom.... independence.... and faith." There was hint of emotion in his voice as he continued, "Faith in myself... faith to go on. But," he said cheerfully, in an attempt to bring the conversation to a close, "most of all love... unconditional love and devotion. That is why," he emphasised, "I have devoted my life to raising funds for the Association, so that others may benefit as I have."

Just then some of the other children, tired of kicking the ball around, also noticed Tom and Bella and headed in their direction.

Suddenly Bella was besieged by a hail of hands and kisses and she was loving every moment of it. Bella was beside herself with excitement. She was everyone's friend and, despite her age, she was every bit as playful as a young puppy. At times like this Tom was convinced that she had never grown up, except when she was in harness and working. She had the gift of bringing sunshine into the lives of the people she met; anyone who made a friend of Bella had a friend for life.

Mr Mason, having finished packing up the remainder of the equipment, made his way over to the group.

"Hello! Tom. All set for next week's marathon, are you?" Tom recognised the games teacher's voice.

"Oh hello, Mr Mason." He tried to control Bella's antics for a moment and commanded her to 'heel'. "Yes!" said the blind man, enthusiastically. "Fighting fit and raring to go, aren't we Bella?" He patted her on the rump and smiled.

"Good!" replied Mr Mason with enthusiasm. "That's what I like to hear." Bella looked up at the games teacher with her bottom wagging as fast as her tail. She wasn't going to let him get away without making a fuss of her first. "Hello there, Bella!" He held her face in his hands and rubbed her ears playfully. "You sound as though you're having a great time with all this attention."

Tom answered, "Yes, she's in her element with all these children around."

"Oh by the way," said the games teacher, letting go of Bella, "I thought you might like to know we are taking a coach party to Barrington the day you finish your marathon so we'll be there to cheer you in on the final stretch."

A broad smile lit the blind man's face. "Oh that's wonderful news." He turned to Bella, "Did you hear that Bella?" he said excitedly. Tom turned once again in the direction of Mr Mason, "Bella and I have been getting in plenty of training by walking a few miles each day, and by now we should be in peak condition," he quickly added, "we hope!"

The games teacher touched Tom on the shoulder in a friendly manner. "Splendid, Tom! Splendid!" Mr Mason looked at his watch before adding "I must go now and round up my flock but..." he took hold of Tom's hand, "Good Luck to you both and don't forget," he said "we'll be rooting for you both."

"It will mean a great deal to Bella and me," answered Tom.

Mr Mason patted Bella lightly on the head as he said his goodbyes and called out to the children. "Come on you lot! It's time we were making tracks back to school." The children reluctantly said their goodbyes to Tom and Bella wishing them luck with the marathon and moved off to collect the games equipment and headed back to school.

* * * * *

Bella looked longingly after the group of children disappearing in the distance. Tom felt for her, "Don't worry Bella," he said, giving her a hug around the neck, "you'll be seeing them all again very soon."

He suddenly realised that the next time would be at the end of the marathon walk and for the first time the enormity of the whole thing hit him. He had been too busy in the last few weeks for any fears to find their way into his thoughts but here, on this wonderful sunny morning, he began to have doubts. Fifty miles doesn't sound very far to walk for a marathon... but to a blind man it was certainly a daunting prospect.

His mind started working overtime. What if they didn't make it. So many people had donated money, equipment; even his walking boots had been donated. And then, of course, there was the media, the sponsors, not to mention the Association.

A sense of panic suddenly overwhelmed him. "Oh Bella!" he said with a heavy heart, "what if....?" Immediately he felt Bella's paw on his knee and a cold damp nose in his hand, and in that moment he experienced again the bond that is unique between a blind man and his guide dog. It was as if Bella sensed his doubts and in her own special way was saying, "Trust me!" Tom hugged her close to him, "Oh Bella! You are my eyes and yet you have no doubt in your heart... so how could I?" Tom's sense of panic was replaced with a feeling of renewed spirit and determination. He stroked his black Labrador with a positive hand. "We'll make it, Bella," he said aloud, as if for the world to hear, "as long as we're together, we'll make it."

Bella took her paw down from his knee, stood up and wagged her tail eagerly, as if to say, "Of course, we'll make it." Her tail was like a barometer for measuring happiness, and right now it was wagging on high.

Tom lifted his face towards the sun. He had learned to gauge the approximate time of day from the position of the sun in the sky. "Come on, Bella," he said, lifting the harness off the seat to place on his guide dog, "it's time for lunch."

CHAPTER TWO: THE STAR ATTRACTION

Saturday, May 12th, dawned and the town of Barrington was greeted with a grey overcast sky that looked like threatening to dampen the spirits of its inhabitants; however, the shops in the High Street were busy preparing for the usual Saturday rush.

Music from internal speakers that were tuned into the local radio station, Radio Westfield, could be heard blaring out from many of the fashion shops for the young, as the assistants busied themselves re-stocking the shelves and the rails before the inevitable onslaught of their Saturday shoppers.

It was nine o'clock and time for the news. Thousands of people were tuned into their radios as John Ainsworth read an up-to-the-minute report of both local and national news. His voice could be heard in the High Street as he reported, "Blind man, Tom Sinclair from Seaton, and his guide dog, Bella, who have been walking for four days now, hope to complete the final stretch of their marathon today. They are expected to arrive in Barrington at two o'clock this afternoon, after a fifty mile marathon to celebrate the Guide Dogs for the Blind Association's Golden Jubilee year, and will have raised many thousands of pounds for the cause.

This remarkable blind man and his guide dog have generated enormous interest and support, both locally and nationally, with their charity walk; reports have been carried by press and TV networks all over the country. As their arrival is expected to attract many well-wishers to the town of Barrington, the police will be closing off part of the High Street for a short time this afternoon. We will keep you in touch with a progress report, so stay tuned won't you? I'll be back with more news at ten o'clock. Now back to Dave Bembow."

"Thank you! John. That was John Ainsworth in our newsroom. We all wish Tom and Bella the best of luck for the remainder of their walk and we look forward to talking to them this afternoon when they finally complete their fifty miles. Marvellous! Now for the Weather Report: After a cloudy start with rain in some parts of the county, the sun is expected to break through this afternoon with temperatures reaching a high of eighteen degrees. So for those of you who have not yet dressed - bikinis and wellies will be the fashion of the day - at least then you'll be half right for half of the day." Dave chuckled wickedly as he continued, "And for all those of you who are still in your beds, here's a song to ease you gently into the morning."

As the morning went on, the High Street filled with shoppers. Saturday mornings were always hectic but today was chaotic; everybody appeared to be getting their shopping done early. With television in almost every home, most people had heard about Tom and Bella. They knew too that their home town of Barrington would be spotlighted in the blaze of publicity set to greet them on their arrival, and that the television cameras, national press reporters and photographers were sure to be there and they didn't want to miss the event.

* * * * *

Tom and Bella had no idea of the amount of excitement they were causing today.

They had set out on their marathon walk on the previous Tuesday morning, starting from Cheadlehulme - which was exactly fifty miles from Barrington - to walk the first ten miles of their journey. This first stage was completed in record time and they stopped overnight in a pre-arranged hotel in Riddlington.

They walked from Riddlington to Abbott's Quay on Wednesday with no major problems. However, the first sign of trouble struck the duo on Thursday morning, when they left their allotted hotel to walk the next ten miles to Brookmarsh.

Starting at eight-thirty in the morning as usual, both

feeling refreshed after a good night's sleep, they made good progress. At the half-way stage, however, clouds loomed on the horizon threatening to soak them and then Bella cut her paw on a carelessly discarded broken bottle.

Tom was unaware of Bella's pain until he thought he detected a slight tug on her harness, as though she was limping. He stopped instantly to check Bella's paws and found she was bleeding quite badly from the right front paw and yet she had not flinched with pain at all. Tom felt much admiration for his guide dog's courage that he wanted to hug her there and then. However, he was aware that she needed instant attention if they were to complete their day's walk. He immediately signalled to the police escort vehicle that he knew was travelling at a discreet distance behind them.

As he waited for the police car to catch up, he reassured Bella but worried thoughts filled his own mind. Would the walk have to be postponed? Or worse.... cancelled? Tom thought about all the preparations being made for them. He had been told that the Mayor of Barrington was to head a large reception in their honour. He also knew that the media would have been arranged in advance. Then he remembered the party of schoolchildren and Mr Mason from Seaton, they would be so disappointed. Then Tom closed his mind to all these negative aspects and told himself, "Bella comes first!"

In no time at all Bella had been treated by the local vet, who retrieved a nasty splinter of glass from her paw, and then placed an antiseptic dressing and bandage over it. The vet assured Tom that the cut was not as bad as the bleeding had suggested. He then recommended that a couple of hours' rest would be sufficient before continuing the four or five miles walk for the day.

It had only been a surface cut but it certainly gave Tom quite a scare. Bella was keen to complete her walk that day and with a few more rest stops than usual they finally arrived at their hotel in Brookmarsh where, although tired and weary, Tom was delighted to find a vet on hand to attend to Bella's dressing before she retired for the night.

After a good night's sleep the lovable Bella was up and willing her partner out of bed, and on with their fourth day's walk to Haysham which they managed without any further hitches, although they arrived at their hotel in Haysham two hours later than scheduled due to Tom's insistence of more rest stops for Bella.

Now the walk was beginning to take its toll on Tom, by now he had blisters on his own feet and he was worried about Bella's paw. He knew that without her help he would be helpless. Again a local vet was on hand to tend Bella's paw and reassured Tom that it was healing nicely.

By now Tom was almost too tired to shower and eat his meal, before falling exhausted into bed. All the hotels had been booked well in advance and all had offered to give their services free - all to aid the Guide Dogs for the Blind Association - and in each one Bella had had a bed made up in the same room as Tom.

Tom struggled out of bed early on Saturday morning telling himself that this was "THE DAY." He checked the blisters on his feet which had been causing him considerable discomfort over the last day or so. Bella heard his movements and bounded over to greet him, rubbing her cold nose into the sole of his bare foot.

"Hey! Bella!" he gasped, "that tickles." Tom decided to put fresh plasters on before attempting the day's walk. Bella watched him inquisitively until he had finished, then she put her paw up onto his knee. Her owner sensed right away what she was up to. "Oh! I see!" he said with a smile in his voice, "You want me to check yours too, eh?" He cuffed Bella playfully around the ear. "Come on then, let's take that bandage off."

Bella held her paw up for Tom to unwind the bandage; at the same time her tail was making a good job of brushing the hotel bedroom carpet. Tom continued unwinding the bandage gently while still talking to Bella. If only he could have seen the adoration in her big soft brown eyes as she watched every expression on his face.

Tom felt all around her paw and was happy to be able to tell Bella that it was nearly healed. He sprinkled some antiseptic powder on a new dressing and covered it with a fresh bandage. Fortunately, the vets had kept them supplied with liberal first aid needs.

"Well," he told his guide dog, "we've walked forty miles so far and it hasn't been too bad has it Bella?" He smoothed her head as he spoke and she listened intently as though she understood every word. "We only have ten more miles to go now, so," he insisted, "we are not going to feel our blisters are we? All we are going to do is feel happy. Happy because each mile we walk today, we know will be a countdown to the finishing post." Tom lifted his head and sighed at the prospect of yet another ten miles' walk.

"Barrington Town Hall here we come," he said out loud, then kissed Bella's head. "We are going to make it Bella, we are." Immediately Bella was across the bedroom waiting anxiously at the door. "Now wait a minute Bella," he jested, "we haven't eaten yet and we can't walk ten miles on an empty stomach, now can we?"

After a hearty breakfast, Tom set off with renewed spirits, to walk the last ten miles of their fifty mile marathon. All the hotel staff turned out to wish them Good Luck. It was eight-thirty and walking seemed comparatively easy for the first mile or so but then they began to slow down as Tom's blisters proved to be more of a nuisance than he had anticipated. He was a great believer in psychology and 'mind over matter' and, therefore, he tried to put into practice some of his beliefs.

Tom tried to block the pain of his blisters from his mind by thinking of all the blind people who would benefit from the money raised; about all the happiness Bella had brought him and how his life had changed from the moment they had teamed up. He thought about all the kind people who had given donations and the sponsors, the hotels and staff. He also thought about the old pensioner who had popped an envelope containing £5 through his door together with a note saying, "Please accept this small donation. I'm sorry it is not more, I only have my old age pension but I'm so grateful that I can see to put this through your door. Good Luck and God Bless You both."

It was working. Tom had managed to walk another mile without noticing how painful his blisters were. He was beginning to feel hot and sticky. It was a humid sort of day where the sun seemed to be struggling to peep though the silver mist. Tom stopped to check the time on his Braille watch; it was almost eleven o'clock and he decided it was time to take a half-hour rest and refreshment before getting back on the road again.

It was almost midday when the sun finally did manage to break through. The heat of the midday sun was the last thing that Tom and Bella needed for the last mile or so. They walked a further half-mile and Tom began mopping his brow. "Phew!" Tom said to Bella, easing back on her harness so that she understood to slow down her pace. "This is thirsty work."

Tom stopped a passer-by to ask directions and enquired how many more miles it was to Barrington Town Hall. It appeared they were only one-and-a-half miles from their final destination. He was relieved to know that they had made excellent progress, in spite of his blisters, and they still had almost two hours before their estimated time of arrival, which was 2 p.m. He didn't want to spoil things and arrive before time.

They slowed their pace down to a leisurely walk and although Bella had been trained so that nothing distracted her while she was in harness working, she couldn't help picking up her owner's vibes. She was so attuned to his needs that they possessed a mental telepathy that was unique. Within minutes Bella was guiding her blind owner towards a large building, just off the main road.

"Hey! Bella!" called an anxious Tom, "where are you

taking me?" He trusted his guide dog implicity - she knew a man's watering hole was always a pub - and that's where she was heading. They stopped at the open door, where Tom only needed one whiff of the beer kegs. "Oh... you clever girl, Bella." He said thinking of the thought of an ice-cool shandy. "Come on then," he said eagerly, "no one will miss us for a few minutes and besides, we need it."

The driver of the police car following behind noted Tom's diversion to the pub. He pulled the car into a lay-by just past the pub and waited for Tom's return, and guessed correctly that Tom needed a toilet.

Afterwards, Tom left Bella to rest in the snug while he went up to the bar, taking care in his unfamiliar surroundings, to order a large bowl of cold water and an ice-cold pint of shandy. Tom and Bella's fame had preceded them and the landlord said, "It's on the house, Tom!" He also told Tom that his customers had been collecting for the charity and a cheque would be sent to the Association's local branch early the following week. Tom thanked him, touched by the generosity of people. "Good Luck on the final stretch, Tom."

It was early so the pub was comparatively quiet and the snug was peaceful; they were both grateful for the rest it afforded them. Bella drank her bowl of water without stopping until it was empty. She licked her mouth, not wasting the tiniest drop, and sat down beside Tom to rest her weary head on his lap.

"Poor Bella!" he said stroking her head gently. "You must be feeling worn out, I know I am and the last mile is going to be the longest one." He closed his tired eyes and felt the burning pain from his aching feet. His blisters were now broken and raw. It would be so easy to give up right now..." Bella immediately lifted her head and pushed her nose into his hand as if to say, "Come on, we are not giving up." She then nudged his other hand, acting impatiently. Tom smiled. "All right! Just let me finish my shandy and then we'll go."

Tom suddenly had a thought. Knowing they had just

over one mile to go and if Bella's paw was healed sufficiently, it would be better to arrive without the obvious bandage.

"Come on, Bella, let's have that bandage off. You don't want to arrive looking as if you've been in the wars, do you?" Bella waved her happy tail vigorously, relieved to have the cumbersome bandage removed. It was just one o'clock by Tom's Braille watch as they prepared to leave the pub.

"Good Luck on the final stretch, Tom," called the landlord as they departed.

Leaving the pub they followed the directions of the landlord and headed towards the town centre of Barrington. As Tom passed, the driver of the police car eased his vehicle back onto the road again, at a discreet distance behind Tom and Bella.

* * * * *

A large blue and silver coach pulled into Barrington's bus station and came to a halt alongside two more coaches from Seaton which had brought Tom's friends and supporters from his home town.

"Here we are!" announced the familiar voice of the games teacher, Mr Mason, standing in the gangway of the coach. "There's a cafe across the road if anyone needs refreshments," and in a more serious voice, "We have to be at the Town Hall in twenty minutes, so I suggest we make it sharp."

The children chatted excitedly as they filed off the coach, Jimmy Lucas was the last to leave and asked, "What if Tom and Bella arrive early, Sir?"

"Oh I doubt that," Mr Mason answered, "their walk has been timed each day and I shouldn't think they will be ahead of schedule on the last day; they'll be too tired for that to happen. If you're that worried I suggest you be back here in ten minutes. Go on, off you go!"

"Yes, Sir," said a deflated Jimmy who wished he hadn't bothered to enquire.

The others were waiting and Basher scowled at him, "Why didn't you keep quiet Lucas?" he snarled, "you've lost us ten minutes and I wanted to buy some chips."

"I don't think Mr Mason meant what he said," David intervened, "or he would have told all the others, but we had better hurry or we won't have time for anything."

* * * * *

The weather forecast for the region was right for a change; the afternoon sunshine was welcomed by the people of Barrington. The preparations outside the Town Hall were being finalised and in the park where the celebrations were to continue for the remainder of the day.

Outside the Town Hall the organisers were putting the final touches to the reception table. A white cloth covered the long table and a tray of champagne glasses had been placed alongside the magnum of champagne which had been generously donated by a local wine merchant.

A large bowl of water was being kept cool in the shade of the tablecloth, in readiness for Bella. Loudspeakers were positioned at the side of the Town Hall steps so that the crowds of well-wishers could hear the progress report from the local radio station.

It was 1.30 p.m. and the TV cameras had been set up and the press reporters had arrived. A local school brass band was ready to play Tom and Bella in for the last one hundred yards or so. The police had sealed off the end of High Street and had positioned many extra duty police along the route.

Mr Mason and his party grouped themselves along the road near the Town Hall steps. They had difficulty finding space as the pavements were already packed with people.

"Oh look!" said Melanie, "Look at the dance troupe. I like their costumes." Their outfits were exceptionally colourful and Rosie had to admit that they were spectacular. The dance troupe were waiting at the far end of the High Street; they were to accompany Tom and Bella as a celebration escort.

Barrington had certainly pulled out all the stops in

staging this reception for Tom and Bella, and the afternoon promised even more celebrations. In the local park a large marquee had been erected for drinks and refreshments, and many stalls were being set up with a wide variety of challenges for both children and adults.

In addition to the stalls, there were to be more specialised entertainment with the dance troupe giving a display of their talents. The brass band was to give their rendition of popular tunes of the day and the local police were putting on a display of their dog-handling skills. As the finale, there was the Maypole Dance, performed by Tom's friends, the children from Seaton Junior High School.

When his party were safely grouped together, Mr Mason went off to make himself known to the Mayor of Barrington. He managed to push his way through the crowd and headed up the steps of the Town Hall to the reception area.

"Good afternoon! Mr Mayor." Mr Mason looked a little uneasy. He wasn't exactly sure of the correct way to address the Mayor. "I... er, I thought I should introduce myself. I'm Brian Mason from Seaton Junior High School, Tom and Bella's home town, and I've brought along the Maypole Dancers for the finale of the celebrations, as pre-arranged."

The Mayor looked puzzled for a moment, then he smiled and Mr Mason relaxed a little. "Oh yes, of course, Mr Mason. How do you do?" he said and they shook hands. "You must forgive me but there is so much going on here today, what with the TV cameras and press reporters hovering about." Mr Mason smiled understandingly and the Mayor turned to an immaculately dressed, distinguished looking man, standing behind them with other dignitaries, saying "Sir Richard .." Mr Mason noticed that the man wore a dark blue tie with a dog motif on it. The Mayor then asked Mr Mason, "Have you met Sir Richard Pringle, President of the Guide Dogs for the Blind Association?"

"No! How do you do Sir Richard?"

The President extended his hand saying, "How do you do, Mr Mason? I'm pleased to meet you."

"I'm delighted to meet you too... er." The Mayor quickly realised he hadn't told the President who Mr Mason was and from where. He apologised before explaining that Mr Mason and the children had arrived from Tom's home town, Seaton, and were to perform the Maypole Dance as the finale to the day's celebrations. Mr Mason also told Sir Richard about the children's friendship with Tom and Bella and their efforts in raising money for the Association.

"What a splendid idea," smiled Sir Richard, "we shall certainly look forward to seeing them perform. Perhaps I may meet the children afterwards." He straightened his shoulders and looked out across the gathering crowds around the Town Hall.

Sir Richard Pringle was a retired Major who had since devoted his life to the work of the Guide Dogs for the Blind Association. "I must say, this is a big day for us. Not only because it's our Golden Jubilee year, but because it's the first time in the history of the Association that a blind man and his guide dog have attempted a sponsored walk of this nature."

The Mayor was quick to agree with Sir Richard. "Yes, it certainly will be a marvellous achievement."

Mr Mason concluded, "Well, if anyone has the courage to make it, it's Tom and Bella. Goodbye! Sir Richard. Goodbye! Mr Mayor. I'd better get back to the children." They both said goodbye and Mr Mason made his way back to his group.

The Mayor checked his pocket watch. It was five minutes to two. The Mayor's aide moved to his side and spoke in his ear. His aide, who almost always accompanied him on official duties, asked the Mayor if he wished the radio to be monitored through the loudspeakers now, in order that everyone could hear the progress report. The Mayor nodded his agreement and the aide signalled to the engineer, who was on hand and waiting to proceed with the relayed transmission.

* * * * *

Tom and Bella had slowed down considerably in the heat of the warm May sunshine. To everyone else it was a beautiful day, but it was too hot for Tom and Bella. "Phew! Bella, this is thirsty work," Tom said exhausted. "The Town Hall can't be that far away now, we just have to keep going a little longer."

He paused for a brief stop, taking a water bottle from his pocket he took a long drink and then poured some into the palm of his hand for Bella which she licked gratefully. Tom then mopped his face and brow with one of the refreshing eau-de-cologne paper towels donated by the local chemist. "Ah..., that's better!" he said as he ran the cool towel around the back of his neck. "Bella, my girl, you and I are going to sleep for a week when this is all over." Bella looked up at Tom as if to say, "You mean for a month, don't you?"

The police car pulled alongside them and the driver asked, "Are you OK Tom?" Tom assured him that they were. "You're nearly there, only about another five or ten minutes and then you'll be in the High Street. I'll be just behind you all the way, so don't worry about the traffic." The driver explained the route to Tom and then pulled back.

Someone called out, 'Well done, Tom! You're doing well Bella. Nearly there!" Strangers had been doing this all along the route and it had been a great encouragement to Tom.

"Thanks!" Tom replied. Spurred on by this well-wisher, Tom and Bella walked on slowly for a further five minutes or so before turning the corner which Tom believed would lead them into the High Street. Suddenly, they were deafened by an almighty cheer from the crowd lining the pavement at the other end of the High Street. Tom just couldn't believe his ears and Bella stopped in her tracks to assess the situation somewhat confused for a moment.

Tom put a reassuring hand on her rump. "It's all right Bella. It's for us! They're cheering for us." The weary blind man stood with his guide dog, amazed as he listened to the hundreds of voices shouting.... "COME ON BELLA! COME ON TOM!"

Tom was completely overwhelmed and he felt near to tears, but jubilant at the same time. "They're cheering for us Bella," he said excitedly, "they're cheering for us." Bella instantly picked up her owner's excitement and her happy tail saluted the crowds. In that moment all the blisters, the tiredness, the aching limbs and cramps were forgotten. They were borne along on a wave of sheer magic as they approached the Town Hall.

The brass band struck up and headed out into High Street, followed by the colourful dancers with their batons and pompoms, then came Tom and Bella, with the police escort bringing up the rear.

The crowds were cheering and clapping on all sides and the driver of the police escort car hooting the horn to try to keep back the crowd; the noise was deafening. To Tom's ears it was sheer heaven. The brass band played the music of the well-known song "Welcome Home".

An elated Tom responded by waving his free hand at the crowds of people who were giving him such a magnificent welcome. The children along the route were shouting now for Bella and she was obviously loving every moment. She turned her head from side to side and that happiness barometer of hers, her tail, was on high.

In the heat of the sunshine Tom felt a thrill run down his spine and tears of pure happiness filled his unseeing eyes. He knew this was a moment in his life that would last in his memory forever. He had been told that there would be a reception committee to welcome them in, but this..., this was beyond belief. He savoured every delicious moment as the crowd joined in with the music and sang "Welcome Home." Then the children took up a chant of "We love Bella! We love Bella!" and Tom found himself saying out loud, "This is fantastic... absolutely fantastic."

The Mayor of Barrington, Sir Richard and the other dignitaries were now on their feet listening to the progress report booming out from the loudspeakers. They were well aware that Tom and Bella had entered the far end of High Street and were now approaching them. Then the radio reporter's voice boomed out again...

"The crowds are beginning to close in and follow this remarkable blind man and his guide dog. The duo must be elated at the thought of being almost at the finishing post... as it were. I say 'remarkable' because Bella has been her blind owner's eyes throughout this marathon walk. She has guided him safely through five different towns at ten miles a day, for five gruelling days. That must surely say a great deal for the Guide Dogs for the Blind Association, who train these wonderful dogs, and we could all take a leaf out of Tom's book of courage......

Tom is beginning to show signs of tiredness now but, no doubt, a glass of celebration champagne will revive him. They only have a short distance to go now to complete the final stretch of this marathon which will, indeed, have raised many thousands of pounds for the Guide Dog Association...."

There was a slight pause before the local radio station's reporter continued.... "Here they come! Yes, we can hear the music of the brass band. The atmosphere here is electric and the cheering is gaining momentum. What a marvellous feeling this must be for them both.... And I've just caught sight of a light aircraft overhead with a tail banner.... The message reads, "CONGRATULATIONS – TOM AND BELLA!" What an incredible sight.... the brass band, the dancers behind, and hundreds of people approaching the Town Hall. Somewhere in the middle of it all is Tom and Bella. There! There I've spotted them, with the police escort vehicle. They're completely surrounded." He was getting caught up in the excitement of it all and was having difficulty in holding back his own emotions at this point but continued... "There are dozens of TV and press reporters waiting anxiously to capture what can only be described as a unique piece of history.

The whole town seems to be willing Tom and Bella in on

the home stretch. Flags are waving, banners are flying...
and ... Yes!...." The radio reporter was now having to shout
to be heard above the cheering.... "TOM AND BELLA
HAVE MADE IT! FABULOUS! CONGRATULATIONS!
WELL DONE, TOM AND BELLA!" The excited voice of the
broadcaster was now drowned out by the cheering crowds as
Tom and his leading lady, Bella, reached the Town Hall.

As Tom approached the steps, he heard the sound of
familiar voices and his heart gave a lurch. David, Jimmy,
Melanie, Basher and little Tim, Rosie and Claire; they were
all there shouting their congratulations to Tom and Bella.
They stood behind the police cordon with outstretched arms
and as Tom passed them they bustled to shake his hand and
pat Bella, who was almost beside herself having recognised
the children. Tom was very emotional as he shook hands
with each of them, and he squeezed each hand to let them
know he knew they were there: he was too emotional to
speak, but then there are no need for words between friends.

* * * * *

Tom recognised Mr Mason's voice as he called out, "Well
done, Tom! Congratulations! Terrific!" He ducked under the
boundary tape, patted Bella and held his arm for the blind
man. "I'll see you safely up the steps to the Mayor's table,
Tom," said Mr Mason with pride in his voice. Gratefully,
Tom tucked his hand through Mr Mason's proffered arm.
The PE teacher politely cleared a pathway through the
people extending their congratulations and presented a now
tired and breathless Tom to the Mayor of Barrington, before
returning to the children at the foot of the steps.

After many handshakes and congratulations all round,
Tom was introduced to Sir Richard Pringle, the President of
the Guide Dogs for the Blind Association. He had heard so
much about the Association's President but had no idea he
would be meeting him in person; that was a thrill in itself.

"The Association and myself are so proud of you both,"

said Sir Richard. "How are you feeling, Tom?" He could only marvel at the seemingly good condition of both the man and the dog. While this was going on, Bella had been given the bowl of water which she promptly emptied.

"Phew! Thirsty!" answered Tom, wiping the perspiration from his forehead. Tom was offered a long cool drink and a seat; he wasn't sure which he needed most; he drank gratefully.

Hearing this, the Mayor was quick to seize the opportunity as he was acutely aware that the press and TV cameras were still in action. "Then I have just the thing for that thirst of yours, Tom." He nodded to his aide "Come, let's open the bottle and let the champagne flow." Tom smiled at the very thought of ice cold champagne. The cork from the magnum of champagne made a resounding "POP!" which delighted the crowd, and the Mayor's aide poured the drinks to the sound of applause.

The Mayor picked up Bella's bowl and placed it on the table, saying, "There's some for you too, Bella." He poured some of his own drink into Bella's bowl and then glanced around to make sure everyone had their glass of champagne before starting his speech.

Again the Mayor nodded to his aide, who moved to the microphone and addressed the crowd. "Ladies and gentlemen!" His voice was clear and precise. "Could I have your attention please? The Mayor of Barrington wishes to speak. Thank you!"

The Mayor straightened his robe and made sure his chain of office was clearly visible before stepping forward. He could see the television cameras rolling and wanted to look good on the Six O'clock News.

"Ladies and gentlemen, before we proceed, could we have three cheers for this remarkable blind man, Tom Sinclair, and his faithful guide dog, Bella..Hip! Hip!" and what sounded like the whole town of Barrington replied with a tumultuous "HOORAY!" This was repeated twice more and still the cheering, whistling and clapping continued.

The dignitaries were now all standing in preparation for the toast, and as the Mayor turned to Tom and raised his glass the others followed suit. "I would like to give a toast to Tom Sinclair, his guide dog Bella and to the Guide Dogs for the Blind Association on the occasion of their Golden Jubilee." The VIPs drank to the Mayor's toast, as Tom sat smiling and sipping his ice-cold champagne, feeling much more relaxed now.

Bella sat watching as they drank their champagne. She had not forgotten that she, too, had some poured for her in her bowl. Standing up on her hind legs, she placed her front paws on the table and sniffed the bottle as if to say, "Where's mine then?" Standing there, she was visible to the cheering crowd, television cameras and photographers alike. The Mayor was quick to notice and smiled knowingly. "Bella, my dear, we almost forgot you, didn't we?"

He suddenly had a mental picture of how Bella, drinking champagne at the Mayor's table, would come across on television and moved the bowl towards Bella. She immediately placed her paws on either side of the bowl as the Mayor said jokingly, "Now Bella, we can't give you too much as we know you're not allowed to drink and guide." There was a chorus of chuckles around the table and applause from the crowd. The Mayor continued, "And I know you are not normally allowed to do this, but today is special, so go on Bella drink your champagne."

Bella looked at Tom for permission and Tom sensing her pause, said enthusiastically, "Go on Bella, have some champagne..You deserve it!"

That was all Bella needed. She slurped greedily at the champagne, oblivious to the roar of laughter as her slurping was picked up by the microphone. On a sea of laughter, rained a hail of cheers, and the television cameramen were quick to move in for a close-up of Bella, as did the press photographers; this certainly was a scoop for the front page giving them a field day with their captions.

Bella's head emerged from the bowl, licking her lips and with all the qualities of a star attraction she lifted one of her paws in the air as if saying "More please!" This endeared her even more to her admiring public and they cheered again. Bella was loving every minute of it.

They were still cheering Bella when the Mayor raised his hands in an attempt to gain attention. "Thank you, ladies and gentlemen. I won't keep you long, I promise. I would just like to say a few words.... if I may?" The Mayor continued, "I know you all join with me in congratulating Tom and Bella, for their outstanding achievement."

He paused momentarily as the handclaps and whistles were appreciated. "They set out on a marathon, that I am sure would have daunted many of us, to celebrate the Golden Jubilee year of the Guide Dogs for the Blind Association which will, indeed, have raised many thousands of pounds for the Association. They set out," he reiterated, "with courage and determination on a fifty mile marathon, which has been a complete success..." he found himself having to pause yet again until the applause died down. "And so, it is with great pride and pleasure...," his voice faded as he turned to take the box his aide had ready for him, "I ask you, Tom..., and Bella, to accept our gift: the Freedom of the Town of Barrington."

He opened the box, before shaking Tom by the hand, to reveal a large black key lying ceremoniously on a bed of silver lining. The key was embossed with the Town's crest. There were more cheers as the Mayor handed the black velvet box to Tom.

Tom, suddenly feeling tearful again, was lost for words. The exhaustion, the excitement and nerves had lowered his emotional threshold. He struggled for his composure as he felt the outline of the key in its bed of satin, his sensitive fingers tracing the outline of the crest as he built up a mental picture of it.

The cheering seemed never ending but finally began to

subside and Tom knew he had to find words somehow. The Mayor helped by interjecting, "We are proud to be your host town and we want you to know that you and Bella will always be welcome in Barrington."

Tom turned to face the crowd of people he knew were out there in front of him. "First of all, I would like to thank you all most sincerely for..."

Suddenly, Bella stood up once more and put her paws on the table beside Tom; she wasn't going to be left out. Tom laughed at his excited guide dog, he knew her so well. She was playing to the star treatment she was getting and he wasn't about to spoil things for her. "All right, Bella, you can say 'thank you' too." Tom rubbed Bella's ear playfully and smiled.

*****

He began again, "Bella and I," he said emphasising the words to add to the humour, "would like to thank all you wonderful people for the marvellous reception we have received here today." He shook his head in amazement, "It's been absolutely fantastic. I can't tell you how truly moved I was to hear so many of you lining the streets and cheering for us." He stroked Bella's head lovingly as he spoke, "I have to admit," he sighed, "that over the past five days there were times when it would have been easy for me to give up.... but, Bella kept me going." He hugged Bella for a moment. "Without her, all of this would not have been possible. So, could we have three cheers for Bella... Hip! Hip!" An overwhelming "HOORAY!" filled the air. As it was repeated again and again, Bella continued standing on her hind legs at the table beside Tom, pawing the air with her right paw, her happy tail swishing the Mayor's robe in her excitement. She was in her element and the applause and cheers were deafening, as Tom sat down.

As the cheering subsided the Mayor stepped up, conscious of time and also of Tom's need for refreshment. "Ladies and gentlemen, I would now like to introduce the

President of the Guide Dogs for the Blind Association, who would like to say a few words.., Sir Richard Pringle."

The President of the Association stepped forward, thanking the Mayor. "Ladies and gentlemen, I would like to congratulate Tom and Bella on behalf of the Association because we are very proud of them indeed." Tom smiled, looking a little nervous and tired, as Sir Richard continued... "As you know, this is our Golden Jubilee year, and we feel deeply honoured to have Tom and his guide dog, Bella, mark the occasion in such a way. It proves," he said with sincerity, "just what the Association set out to achieve..fifty years ago, that a guide dog can open up a whole new world to a blind person. Tom and Bella are a splendid example of the team spirit that offers freedom and independence to the blind, not to mention the bond of friendship and love they share." He smiled in admiration at the two of them, then turned to the crowd again. "You know, a blind person without a guide dog is like a ship without a sail. Thank you all for the splendid support you have given Tom and Bella, and the Association, today and over the years. Thank you!"

As Sir Richard sat down there was again applause and the Mayor resumed his position at the microphone. "Thank you, Sir Richard. I would now like to remind you all that celebrations will continue in the park for the remainder of the afternoon, with Tom, Bella and Sir Richard as our special guests." Turning in Tom's direction, the Mayor asked, "Tom, do you feel up to the ten minute walk to the park?"

Tom smiled, the adrenalin was still pumping around his veins keeping fatigue at bay. "Yes!" he said eagerly, "no problem."

"Good!" said the Mayor. He whispered an aside to Tom, "We have a beer tent so you will be able to put your feet up with a nice cool pint."

The thought certainly appealed to Tom. "That sounds wonderful," he said with a lingering sigh.

The Mayor tapped the microphone to make sure it was still working properly before addressing the crowd once more. Again he called for their attention. "Ladies and gentlemen. If you wouldn't mind clearing a path for Tom and Bella, we will try to make our way towards the park where there are refreshments and lots of games and stalls for everyone, so, why not come along and join us. Thank you!"

As the crowd pulled back, the Mayor of Barrington, Tom, Bella, Sir Richard Pringle, followed by all the other VIPs, made their way down the Town Hall steps. The band moved in behind them playing the popular tune, 'Congratulations...' Then came Mr Mason, David, Claire, Rosie, Jimmy and their friends from Tom's home town of Seaton. They were followed by hundreds of well-wishers. Soon there was a procession stretching for half a mile or more, with Tom and Bella leading it. It was like a scene from the 'Pied Piper' and Bella was certainly calling the tune: this was her moment of glory, walking with her tail and her head held high as if she had been born to lead.

Tom was still riding high on the excitement of it all, although every step he took caused him pain from the broken blisters on his feet but he knew they would soon heal. Tom lifted his joyful face to the sun and checked its position: the rays touched his cheekbone and he judged it to be about three o'clock. "Who cares what time it is," he said to himself, " there are still a few hours of this wonderful day left to enjoy; I'll have plenty of time to rest up tomorrow."

Tired, but jubilant, Tom and Bella headed the procession and Tom felt so very proud. "This," he told himself, "is a day I will remember for the rest of my life."

CHAPTER THREE: A LASTING IMPRESSION

The month of October had crept up on Tom, catching him by surprise. He shivered as he turned up the collar of his raincoat against the chill east wind. The park seemed deserted as they walked through a bed of rustling leaves. Bella loved the sensation of sinking into a sea of feathery softness.

Barrington and the charity walk seemed a long time ago and yet... still close to their hearts. The remembrance of the wonderful welcome they had been given, gave the blind man a warm glow inside - a glow that would forever warm him on the coldest of days. He reflected on the success of it all and a smile crossed his face. Bella was now famous and she had become a household name and was very much in demand.

Since the walk, Bella's pictures had graced the front covers of magazines both at home and abroad and the affable guide dog had become a star at press interviews and photo sessions. Hardly a day went by when the phone didn't ring, enquiring if Bella would be available to open a fete or to attend some event to accept a cheque on behalf of the Guide Dogs for the Blind Association.

Tom was also in demand to give talks about the work of the charity; in fact, that was where they were off to this chilly morning. This famous duo were getting star treatment and life was just wonderful.

Bella responded to Tom's command to stop, and he felt his Braille watch. "Ten to nine! Not too bad," he said aloud. He patted Bella affectionately, then gave the 'forward' command.

"We should be there by nine," he told himself as he paced his walk briskly, to keep warm. There was a ruddy glow forming on Tom's cheeks, nose and chin, which made his handsome face take on a more youthful appearance.

Tom loved the exhilaration of a brisk walk, and only Bella gave him the confidence to do that. The lighthearted sense of freedom meant so very much to this grateful owner of a very special guide dog.

He could hear the leaves spinning through the air and falling at his feet in their last brave attempt to dance in defiance of nature. Tom couldn't help thinking what a sad time of year autumn was and he tried to picture the cherry blossoms that would have been a delight in the spring. He thanked God he hadn't been born blind. At least he had his memories and they were as clear and sharp as ever. He polished his memories every day by building mental pictures of all the details his other senses offered him.

Tom much preferred the spring: spring was so vibrant, so full of colour, so full of life. But then he mused philosophically, "If we didn't have the changing seasons, we wouldn't have the spring to look forward to each year... and besides, it's nature's way of turning the cycle of life."

As they made their way through the park, they turned into the avenue of almost bare cherry trees that Tom knew would lead them directly to the main gates.

"Good girl, Bella," said Tom as they approached the gates. "You know the way, don't you?" Tom had been invited to give a talk on the Guide Dogs for the Blind Association at Seaton's Comprehensive School. He had chosen to go through the park as the route was so much quicker than going through the town itself, especially with so many people now recognising them and stopping for a friendly chat.

On arrival at the school, Tom and Bella were taken to the main hall, where an assembly was held each morning. Today's talk was to be an extension of the assembly. The children, as always, made a huge fuss of Bella and she needed no coaxing to reciprocate and so the children were hardly in a reverent mood for prayers when the headmaster entered the hall and called for quiet. Tom and Bella were invited to join the headmaster on the raised platform at the front of the assembly hall.

"Good morning, children!" said the headmaster.

The children replied with the customary "Good morning, Sir!"

Mr Clevely then read a short prayer and as the children sat down he said, "We are very fortunate to have with us this morning, Mr Sinclair and his guide dog, Bella, who, I might add, have become celebrities since we last had the privilege of their company. I expect you've all read about them in the newspapers." There was a murmuring of "Yes" and nods of agreement. Mr Clevely smiled at the response.

"Now that prayers are over, Mr Sinclair would like to give a talk on the work of the Guide Dogs for the Blind Association, and all the marvellous work they do."

Mr Clevely turned to Tom and smiled, "The floor is all yours, Mr Sinclair."

Tom fidgeted with Bella's harness handle, as if he were a little uncomfortable. He always was somewhat nervous at the start of these talks, but within seconds of beginning to talk about the work of the Association, he was unstoppable.

He looked in the direction he knew the children to be and lifted his head high as he spoke. "Good morning, children!" he said cheerfully and back came a chorus of "Good morning, Mr Sinclair!.... Good morning!" Tom thought it sounded as though there were a hundred or more in the room, but it was difficult to tell exactly. He let Bella's harness rest, which was the cue for the obedient guide dog to settle down beside her owner while the spotlight was on him.

"I'm delighted to have been invited back here to your lovely school. If you remember the last time we had a talk, I explained how the Guide Dog movement was started and how it had progressed over the past fifty years. Well?" he said with a question mark hanging over the word, synonymous with many of Tom's introductory paragraphs, "Today I would like to talk about fundraising, and what happens to all the money, so generously donated by the public."

There was a slight pause while he waited for a couple of

bottoms to finish shuffling on the floor, then Tom proceeded in earnest.

"Each dog costs approximately one thousand pounds to train as a guide dog. In fact, they cost very much more than that but we say one thousand pounds because it is a nice round figure to work on. Now, that doesn't mean to say," he was quick to point out, "that that is the price a blind person has to pay for their guide dog. On the contrary, all a blind person has to contribute is a token payment of fifty pence. I will explain the reason for that in a moment." He paused again to take a breath before explaining how the money was actually used.

"Now, how is the money used in relation to costs, you might ask. Well, I will tell you. To make it easier for you to understand I will explain how each pound of the charity money is spent. Out of every one hundred pence, fifty-two pence is spent on breeding, puppy-walking and training a guide dog. A further twenty-two pence is spent on after-care, guide dog feeding allowance and veterinary fees."

As he paused for breath, Tom could have heard a pin drop, and he knew he had the children's full attention now.

"Another nineteen pence goes towards the maintenance and depreciation of the many guide dog training centres around the country and lastly," he stressed, "seven pence goes towards administration costs. So, there we have it... fifty-two pence, twenty-two pence, nineteen pence and seven pence adds up to a total of one hundred pence. Of course," explained Tom, "the percentage is the same for a thousand pounds."

Bella began to fidget, throwing darting glances at the children sitting in the front row. She loved her trips to school but wasn't so keen on the talks, mainly because the children had to be quiet and couldn't play with her. She stood up and then flopped down on the floor again beside her master with a mini-grunt, settling herself into a more comfortable position.

Suddenly, something caught Bella's eye and her ears

twitched while the rest of her body lay motionless. Mr Clevely, the headmaster, was stood on the other side of Tom, with his head down and hands clasped in front of him, listening intently to what the blind man was saying. He was unaware that his white handkerchief was protruding from his pocket, or that Bella had noticed.

Bella had a thing about handkerchiefs, she simply adored pulling them out of people's pockets or 'fishing' for them in ladies' handbags. She was dying to have a bit of fun but she wasn't too sure of the reaction she would get from Mr Clevely. Eventually, the lovable black Labrador decided to behave herself and just heaved a big sigh as her owner continued his talk.

"The Guide Dogs for the Blind Association doesn't get any help from the Government. Therefore," he said hoping to get this particular message over to all his listeners, "they rely entirely on the generous support of the public. There are at least seven training centres around the country and a breeding centre who have almost six thousand dogs on their books."

Tom went on to explain, "Now, of this six thousand dogs, two hundred and fifty dogs are breeding stock, eight hundred are puppies, six hundred and fifty dogs are in training, and as many as three thousand seven hundred are working dogs and, of course," he said hopefully, "these numbers will increase as time goes on. I must also mention, there are a further five hundred or more retired guide dogs. Now that sounds as though the Guide Dog Association have a tremendous number of dogs in their care, and certainly they have. But!" he pointed out, "they need many more if they are to help all the blind people around the country..and that means a great deal of money has to be raised in order to do this."

Bella with her chin resting on the wooden floor, looked hopefully at the children then at the tempting handkerchief in Mr Clevely's pocket that was almost saying, 'Come and get

me, Bella'. Her ebony eyes darted from one to the other hoping for a sign of encouragement from the children but, no, they were too interested in what the 'boss' had to say.

"I don't know if many of you know this, but the average life of a working dog is seven to eight years and so the Association have to train five hundred guide dogs every year.... just to replace retired guide dogs. Also," he said, as a little light went on in his memory, "I said I would explain about the nominal charge of fifty pence which a blind person pays. Well now, as the Association's funds come entirely from voluntary donations from the public, they make only a token charge of fifty pence when they hand over the trained guide dog to its new owner. This allows the blind person to retain a little pride in the fact that he has contributed to the cost of his or her dog. This contribution goes towards administration costs." Again Tom paused for breath before going on....

"The Association also give a feeding allowance, after care and pay any veterinary costs, in order to ensure that all blind owners can afford to keep their guide dog healthy." Once again Tom stressed, "And the more funds that are available.... the more blind people we can help!"

Tom paused, he couldn't quite make out why there were giggles coming from the children in front of him. Suddenly, the giggles exploded into laughter. Instinctively, the blind man put his hand down to feel where his guide dog should have been sitting quietly, but now wasn't. "Oh no!" he thought, "What's Bella up to now?"

Mr Clevely, unaware of the reason, was not amused at the laughter. A frown deepened in his forehead as he clapped his hands in an attempt to gain control of the situation. "Could we please have silence, Mr Sinclair is trying to talk and cannot possibly be heard above this gaggle of giggles." The headmaster looked a little embarrassed at his choice of words.

A young boy at the front put his hand up. "Please Sir!" he giggled, "Bella's got your handkerchief."

Mr Clevely immediately put his hand into his pocket where he knew there was a white handkerchief, he'd put it there clean only this morning, and yes.... it had gone! To the embarrassment of the headmaster of Seaton Comprehensive School, the whole assembly burst into laughter.

Tom closed his eyes, thinking "Oh no!"

Mr Clevely feeling in his other pocket caught sight of Bella peering round the back of Tom's legs, looking more than a little sheepish. She stared up at the headmaster with her big 'don't tell me off' eyes, with the evidence still dangling from her mouth. When Bella looked at you with those eyes she could melt an iceberg and Mr Clevely laughed out loud, his handkerchief looking startlingly white against the ebony black fur of Bella's coat, "So, you're the culprit," he joked.

Tom put his hand down to where he knew he would find the headmaster's handkerchief. "BELLA!" he scolded, "that's naughty!" The black Labrador's tail crept between her hind legs; she hated being told off. To her a harsh word was much worse than any other form of punishment. "Now!" said Tom, "you give that handkerchief back to Mr. Clevely. At once! Go on!" he insisted.

With her tail still between her legs, Bella walked slowly over to the headmaster and dropped the now slightly creased handkerchief into his extended hand. Mr Clevely rubbed her ears affectionately, "Thank you, Bella." he said looking into her pleading eyes, "It's all right, I forgive you. But!" he shook his head, "I must say you were very clever.... I didn't feel a thing."

Bella was happy to know she was not in disgrace and wagged her tail thankfully.

The children smiled in admiration at Bella's ability to 'get one over' on their headmaster. They had watched her eyeing up his handkerchief while Tom was talking, until she couldn't resist the temptation any longer.

Tom was most apologetic. "I'm terribly sorry," he said to

the smiling headmaster. "I do hope she hasn't spoiled it for you. I'm afraid Bella has a soft spot for handkerchiefs."

A warm smile lit the whole of Mr Clevely's face, "No, she hasn't spoiled it. In fact, she's given us all a jolly good laugh to start the day."

Order was restored once more and a relieved Tom asked the children if they had any questions. However, the awkward silence that followed told Tom that the lack of feedback was due to the cabaret act that Bella had decided to add to their visit and concluded, "Well, thank you all for listening. Thank you for being interested in the work of the Guide Dogs for the Blind Association. It has been a privilege to be invited back, yet again, to your school."

Mr Clevely then addressed the assembly, "I would like to thank Mr Sinclair... and Bella! for coming along this morning to give us a most interesting and, may I say.... most entertaining talk." He smiled in the direction of Tom and Bella and added, "We look forward to seeing you both again in the near future."

The whole assembly of children and teachers applauded as Mr Clevely shook hands with Tom and thanked him personally, and then rubbed Bella's ears affectionately again.

The children made a great fuss of Bella on their way out of the hall. Bella was sad to see them go, and while they made their way to their various classrooms the headmaster accompanied Tom and Bella as far as the school gates.

* * * * *

The morning seemed to be taking a long time to warm up thought Tom as the cheeky wind nipped the lobes of his ears. He felt his watch which told him it was nine-forty-five. He stood momentarily undecided which route to take home, but the cold wind made up his mind for him. "Come on, Bella!" he said, bracing himself for the walk, "Let's go home the way we came."

Turning through the park gates, they once more walked through the rustling leaves. Tom smiled to himself at Bella's

antics back at school. "Bella, my girl," he teased, "you really must learn to control yourself when you see hankies sticking out of people's pockets... you'll get me into trouble one of these days." Bella looked up at him as if say, 'Never!'

The park was one of Bella's favourite places. She looked longingly in the direction of the playing fields, but there was no sign of any children. The dried leaves underfoot continued to rustle as they bounded off Tom's shoes, and Bella kicked at the fluffy leaves underfoot - a minor distraction.

The sound of ducks and geese grew louder telling tom that they were past the avenue of cherry trees and now walking alongside a tall perimeter hedge that separated the lake from the path. Bella pricked up her ears at the call of a more unusual species, but soon relaxed as she identified it as a duck.

Tom was still lost in thoughts about the events of the morning, when suddenly, he stepped into a nightmare.

The unsuspecting blind man froze with fear as he heard the frantic rustling coming from the bushes beside him. His face turned a peculiar shade of grey and the feeling of imminent danger sent a cold chill down his spine. Fear fixed him to the spot; the hair on Bella's back rose and Tom heard a low growl in the back of her throat.

Suddenly, Tom felt the full weight of a man's body pounce on him from behind. An arm grabbed him around the throat, filling his nostrils with the stale smell of oily leather and cigarette smoke. Before he could even try to retaliate, he was forced into a lock position, unable to move a muscle. He felt something, which he took to be a knife, pressed against his back. An aggressive voice, reeking of alcohol, yelled from behind his ear, "Hand over your money blind man... or you're dead" Tom winced as he felt the knife press into his back. He had no doubt that this madman meant what he said.

In the second that this happened, Bella was fastening

her mouth around the arm that held Tom in its grip. She took the man by surprise and within seconds had forced him to the ground. A stunned Tom heard the sound of metal hit the path and felt relief that, at least the menacing knife was out of the way. He stood there helpless. He could hear Bella struggling with his assailant on the grass beside him. Adrenalin was pounding around his body in readiness to defend himself. But, he agonised, how can I fight what I cannot see. "Oh God!" he cried out in frustration and, in a rare moment, he cursed his blindness.

Bella braced herself against the blows that seemed to be coming from all directions.... she was determined to hold on. Her attacker suddenly broke free and tried to run, but Bella wasn't going to let him get away. She pounced again, this time going for a more vulnerable part of his body. She seized his hand and pinned him down to the ground, holding the greasy-haired youth in a vice-like grip. In a desperate attempt to free himself he tried to tear his hand from her jaw with such force that her teeth penetrated the skin. He let out an almighty yell that resounded around the empty park but still Bella held on.

Suddenly, as if Tom's prayers had been answered, he heard footsteps running towards them. "Hey! What's going on there?", yelled the voice of a man of mature years.

The youth heard the shout and began to panic even more. Kicking out wildly he caught Bella in the ribs. She squealed and was momentarily winded. Tom held his breath fearing for his guide dog and yet.... helpless to assist! The attacker broke free of the winded Bella at last and ran like a rocket.... through the bushes, across the grass and into the distance.

Bella's natural instinct was to give chase, which she did. As soon as Tom realised, he shouted after her and her training at the Guide Dog Centre paid off, and she returned to heel.

Tom was still in a state of shock, hugging his beloved Bella, when the man who had shouted finally caught up with them. Out of breath and wheezing, the stranger gasped, "Are you all right?"

Tom detected the voice of an elderly man, suffering from bronchial trouble by the sound of it. "Yes! I think so" said a dazed Tom. As he stood up Tom caught the distinct smell of sheepskin leather and mothballs, obviously the man's coat had only just come out of summer hibernation.

"I saw what happened," said the man puffing and panting, "I was on the other side of the park but I'm afraid I couldn't run very fast. I suffer from Bronchitis." The stranger's breathing was becoming less laboured as he bent to retrieve the knife from the ground, suddenly remembering he would be wise to use a handkerchief with which to pick it up, as valuable fingerprints could be on the handle. He looked at the menacing knife and then at Bella saying, "It looks as though your dog saved your life."

Tom's senses were slowly returning, "Yes! She saved my life all right."

The stranger had a kind voice and Tom felt somewhat comforted. "She must be quite a dog," he said, stroking the panting guide dog. Tom felt proud to be able to tell him her name was Bella. "Not THE BELLA!" exclaimed the stranger, "Not the Bella we've been reading about in the papers?"

"That's the one!" said Tom. He could almost hear the stranger shaking his head.

"Well! Well! Well!" he said in amazement. He gave a rasping cough before continuing. "Well, now, we ought to be thinking about getting you to the police station to report this." He looked at the still visibly shaken blind man asking, "Do you feel up to it?"

Tom had to admit that he felt much more in need of getting safely home for a hot cup of tea and a warm by the fire. However, he was sensible enough to know that if he failed to report this attack to the police, the youth would be free to attack again.

After a much needed cup of tea, statements were taken at the police station and the stranger went on his way, while Tom and Bella were taken home in a police car.

Home for Tom and Bella was a modest semi-detached, red brick house in Portland Road, consisting of two bedrooms and a bathroom upstairs, and a lounge and dining room downstairs with a well-equipped kitchen, which had been 'geared' to cater for Tom's particular needs.

Tom used the dining room as a sitting room as well, as it was convenient to the kitchen. It had a cosy feel about it, with two ample fireside chairs either side of the electric fire. An ornate clock on the mantlepiece chimed the hour and every half-hour. A solid oak table and four chairs occupied the centre of the room, with a bowl of fresh fruit placed neatly in the middle of it, while in the corner was Tom's lifeline - the telephone - standing on a small table covered in a white Nottingham lace cloth.

An olive shade of green dominated the striped linen curtains hung at the window which framed a neatly edged lawn, with the last of the summer roses still in bloom around the borders. It certainly was a well-kept garden which would have put many sighted people to shame. The opposite wall boasted a large antique sideboard, full of framed photographs of Bella mostly meeting some famous person or other. This was one of Tom's greatest pleasures in life, to show these pictures off to his visitors. He was so proud of his friend and constant companion, Bella, his guide dog.

Tom felt a sense of relief as he unlocked the back door to his home. They always used the back entrance where Tom kept a bowl of fresh water waiting for Bella on their return, which she was always ready for and today was no exception. Tom took off her harness and Bella made straight for her bowl. Her weary owner went to switch the fire on in the living room before putting on the kettle to make himself a cup of tea.

As Tom sat sipping his tea by the fire, Bella made herself comfortable in her favourite place, on a hearth rug at her owner's feet in front of the fire. The warmth was comforting and soon she was asleep, snoring softly. Her ordeal earlier in the day had worn her out.

Reflecting on all that had happened, Tom could hardly believe it. Bella had saved his life, there was no doubt about that. He shuddered at the thought of what might have happened had he only had a white stick to rely on: it didn't bear thinking about.

He let his hand drop down the side of the armchair and lovingly stroked Bella. This soothing action and the sound of Bella snoring peacefully, calmed his troubled mind and he drifted into a state of relaxation. The rhythmic ticking of the clock above the fire helping to lull him into blissful sleep.

Tom jumped with fright as the shrill ring of the telephone rang repeatedly, sounding more like church bells pealing in his head. Bella was immediately on her feet. "It's all right Bella," said Tom trying to think straight. As he lifted the receiver, Bella was at his side wagging her tail hopefully. She had learned to associate the telephone calls with the charity work to which she and Tom had dedicated their days.

"Hello! Mr Sinclair?" The voice sounded familiar. "It's Mike Bretton from the Evening Chronicle."

Tom tried to stifle a yawn as he spoke, "Hello! Mike."

"We've just had news of the attempted mugging this morning. Are you both OK?"

"Yes, thank the Lord. We're all right."

"I hear Bella saved your life, is it true?"

Tom was beginning to think a little better now, "Yes!" he said... "Yes! It's true. But for Bella I might not be here talking to you on the 'phone. It was... It was frightening, to say the least."

"Look, Mr Sinclair," he said, checking the time on his watch, "I know it's twelve thirty and getting near lunchtime, but could I come to your house now? You see I'd like to get a photograph of you and Bella, and get this story in tonight's paper."

"Yes, of course you can." He hadn't realised the papers would be getting hold of the story; he'd hardly had time to take it in himself.

"Great!" said Mike, "I'll be there in about ten minutes."

Tom thought the young reporter sounded as if he'd just scooped the story of the day. He shook his head and said out loud, "It could well have been but for you, Bella."

Mike knew Tom fairly well. He had interviewed him on a number of occasions in connection with the charity work and, as always, Bella was happy to have her photograph taken; the press always took more shots than they needed.

The blind man didn't mind too much giving his own account of the incident, but he was amazed at how frightened he felt as he recalled the details. He tried to think of the positive side of the whole ghastly experience. He told Mike that without doubt Bella had proved that a guide dog was so much more than a pair of eyes, so very much more.

With the story complete, Mike left hurriedly, to get back to the office before the paper went to print. Tom didn't feel like food but managed some soup before settling down once more beside the fire with Bella.

The clock ticked away in the background but Tom just couldn't settle, too many thoughts were running through his mind. He felt a strange mixture of nervous tension: anger, fear, sadness, apprehension. He knew it was going to take a long time to get over the shock. These anxieties would have to be tackled one at a time, so that they wouldn't overcrowd his mind and cause confusion, but for the moment all he wanted was to relax.

He put his hand down the side of his chair, where Bella lay. A cold wet nose pushed into his hand told him she wasn't able to sleep either. As if thinking his thoughts out loud he said, "Don't worry, Bella, we're not going to let this morning spoil our walks in the park... we'll go tomorrow." Bella was up immediately, nudging her owner's hand and wagging her tail. "No! Not now, Bella... tomorrow." He smoothed her head reassuringly making a conscious decision that this incident was not going to curtail his freedom.

The remainder of the afternoon turned out to be far from peaceful. "News travels fast, Bella," said Tom as he went to answer yet another call. It hadn't taken long for other papers to get hold of the story and there were more interviews and photographs.

Just as Tom reached his favourite chair again, the doorbell rang three times. Bella jumped up excitedly, her tail slapping at Tom's legs as he went to answer the door, which told Tom it wasn't a stranger. He felt his Braille watch, "Who can this be, Bella?"

The door opened to reveal an anxious David and Jimmy. "Hello!" said David, "Its David and Jimmy."

"Oh hello, boys!" said Tom, trying desperately to control his very excited black Labrador. "This is a pleasant surprise. Do come in."

It took David and Jimmy a minute or two to calm Bella down; she was so excited and nearly smothered the boys with affection. David then explained, "The reason we've called is to see if you are all right."

Jimmy was quick to add, "We've just seen the evening paper, saying.... 'Guide dog, Bella, saves owner from vicious attack.' Is it true, Tom?"

"Yes, it's true I'm afraid," said Tom, ushering them into the living room. "Come and sit by the fire and I'll tell you about it."

David asked in a concerned voice, "Whatever happened?"

Bella settled at last alongside Tom's chair, while he recounted the full story of all that had happened that day.

"Well!" exclaimed an impressed Jimmy, "You're a hero now, Bella." From her horizontal position, Bella wagged her tail at Jimmy with a resounding thud.

"Shouldn't that be 'heroine'?" enquired David.

"You can call her what you like," said an admiring Jimmy, "But in my book she's a hero!"

David looked at Tom as he smiled at Jimmy's comment, "Do you think the police will catch the man who attacked you?"

"Oh yes!" said Tom, "I'm sure they will. Bella made quite an impression on him, from the yell he let out!"

The two boys laughed and Jimmy added, "Good for you, Bella."

The clock chimed and David suddenly realised the time, "Sorry, Tom, it's six o'clock, we'd better be getting back home for tea."

Jimmy agreed, "Yes, my mum will be sending out a search party for me if I don't hurry." He turned to Tom, "Are you sure you will be all right on your own, Tom? We could come back later... as long as my mum knows where I am she won't mind."

"I'll be all right boys, thanks for offering," said a very grateful Tom.

David, preparing to leave, said, "We'll call in again in a day or two to see how you are."

Tom thanked the boys for their concern, and for calling to see him. Bella sat at the front door beside Tom, with her great big 'hound dog' eyes saying she was sorry to see them leaving so soon.

Jimmy couldn't resist that look in her eyes. "It's all right, Bella," he said smoothing her troubled brow, "We'll come and see you again soon." Before he left he whispered in her ear, "You go in and look after Tom, after all you're the hero now."

Tom waved goodbye to the boys and closed the door on the chill wind. It was going to be a long evening he told himself, but perhaps they could catch up on the rest they had been trying to get all afternoon. "Come on, girl!" he said, "Time for your tea." Bella pricked up her ears and wagged her tail as she followed Tom into the kitchen. Tom was always careful to stick to a strict timetable where Bella's food was concerned; after all she was expected to have regular toilet habits, as were all guide dogs.

Bella, like all Labrador's, loved her food and ate lustily from the bowl Tom put down for her. After a trip to the garden, she settled down for the evening beside Tom. The warmth of the fire was comforting and conducive to the peaceful nap they were both enjoying when... yes, you've guessed!... the telephone rang piercing the silence. "Oh no! It's just not my day today," said Tom.

CHAPTER FOUR: THE LIGHT OF MY LIFE

The traffic lights were showing red and Bella came to a halt at the kerb. She sat and waited patiently with Tom until the lights changed to green and the traffic stopped at the crossing. Tom knew the sounds and the smells of the town all too well - he recognised the sound of a double decker bus, private cars and heavy goods vehicles; and the smell of freshly baked bread told the blind man that he was in Kimberley Street in Seaton town centre.

Tom heard the sound of compressed air brakes, accompanied by the smell of diesel oil and a jolt on the harness as Bella stood up, waiting to take him safely across the busy main road. Once they were across Tom breathed in the smells from the various shops until he found the one he was happy to recognise, the aroma of freshly ground coffee emanating from Giovanni's Coffee Shop, and there was a smile on Tom's face as he spoke to Bella. "It isn't far now, Bella." Bella knew they never went to town without calling at the coffee shop for their regular cup of coffee and a cream slice. This was Tom's special treat, once a week.

It was a damp November day, making it feel colder than it actually was, but there was a rush of warm aromatic air as they entered Giovanni's. Bella guided Tom to his usual table.

"Good morning! Mr Sinclair. Good morning! Bella." Tom recognised the voice as its owner went on, "And how are you today?"

"Good morning! Antonio, we're fine thank you."

The Italian waiter continued, "What can I get you this morning. A coffee and Viennese slice?"

"Yes, please," said Tom, rubbing his hands together in anticipation.

The waiter was quick to add, "But NO for Bella? I remember, Sir!"

Tom smiled as he confirmed, "That's right, Antonio, none for Bella." Tom heard Antonio walk away, then the rattle of cups and saucers, and remembered telling the generous Antonio that guide dogs were trained not to accept food or titbits of any kind, while they were working and in harness. He'd explained that a blind person's life depended on their guide dog and if they were at any time distracted, especially crossing a busy road, by some well-meaning person with a biscuit or sweet, the results could be disastrous. Consequently, Antonio reminded himself each time he saw Bella or, indeed, any other working guide dog. Tom never felt he was denying Bella, for she had her fair share of treats at home.

Bella sat patiently until Tom had finished his treat. As soon as he had finished she stood up, wagging her tail. "All right, Bella," teased Tom, "I know you're anxious to get to the park, but," he warned, "I'm not sure the children will be there... It might be too cold for them now." He felt the cool draught from Bella's wagging tail stop. "Well it is November, Bella." She looked up with pleading eyes before bringing her chin to rest on his knee, she knew her friend so well. "Still," he said, "they might just be there," and his voice seemed to lift along with Bella's spirits.

Tom paid his bill and thanked Antonio before exchanging the warmth of the cosy cafe for the cold dampness of Kimberley Street.

Tom found himself walking through a few lingering autumn leaves and the rustling sound from underfoot together with the eerie silence of the deserted park sent a chill down his spine. It triggered off a memory of the attack, just over a month ago, which he wanted so much to forget. He pushed the unwelcome thoughts to the back of his mind with the thought that the incident was now in the past and it was the future that mattered. He straightened his shoulders resolutely as he walked on.

Bella's ears strained back to sharpen her hearing and as Tom felt the movement he became aware of children's voices drifting across the park, as they neared the Dingle. "It sounds as if you might be in luck, Bella." The excited

Labrador quickened her pace, hoping her owner wouldn't notice. "Steady now, Bella," he said, with a slight tug on the harness reminding her of the pace at which she had been trained to walk. Bella obeyed instantly. "All in good time... All in good time," Tom assured her.

Continuing to guide her owner to his usual park seat, Bella's tail started wagging excitedly as the children's voices grew louder. Tom felt the seat before sitting down; he was used to finding an assortment of bags and coats..even lunch boxes, and today was no different. He cleared himself a space and sat down. Bella's tail was now waving frantically as she watched the children, who, as yet, hadn't seen her: they were engrossed in their games. Tom relaxed her harness and kept her on a short lead.

Suddenly the children spotted them. A voice, sounding very much like Jimmy's, called out, "Hey! Look! There's Bella!" Within minutes the children crowded round their favourite dog.

Her bemused owner sat smiling to himself, he knew what to expect. There was something special about this guide dog. She was like a burst of sunshine on a grey day. She possessed qualities that could neither be bought nor sold; like faith, trust, devotion, companionship, friendship, but most of all.... love. Bella generated the kind of love that could melt the heart of a snowman. She endeared herself to all age groups but especially the children.

David was the first to break away from the Bella Fan Club and say hello to Tom. "Hello! David. We weren't sure if you'd be here today."

"We talked 'nicely' to Mr Mason and he let us come for a game of football." Mr Mason was busy giving extra tackling lessons to some of the less agile players. "You normally stop coming around this time of year, don't you?" asked Tom as he struggled to hold on to the excited Bella's lead.

"Yes! That's right!" said David as he pushed some of the bags further along the seat and sat down, "His is the last time we come until the spring."

Tom sighed and glanced in the direction of his charge. "I don't know what Bella is going to do.... She's going to miss all the attention. Look at her, she's in her element."

David laughed saying, "You'll have to send her to school, Tom."

Suddenly a chirpy voice came from nowhere. "Hello! Tom." It was Jimmy; Tom recognised his voice instantly.

"Hello! Jimmy, how are you today?"

"I'm fine thanks," said Jimmy, as he shivered against the cold wind and tried to warm up his circulation by running on the spot. "Brr! It's a bit nippy today isn't it?" Tom agreed.

"Still," said Jimmy breathlessly, "at least it's not raining. Last year Bonfire Night was a washout."

"Oh, of course," said Tom as he realised, "I'd forgotten it was Bonfire Night."

David, still bemused by Bella's antics, added, "Bonfire Night isn't what it used to be. I don't think so anyway."

Tom laughed, "You sound like an old man, David."

"No, but you know what I mean." David sat absent mindedly splitting a piece of grass between his thumb and index finger. "People don't seem to bother like they used to, do they?"

Claire, who had overheard David, chipped in, "That's probably a good thing," she said, making herself room to sit down beside Tom. "Too many people have been injured with fireworks and bonfires." She went on in her grown-up voice, "Perhaps one day they will ban it altogether, what do you think, Tom?"

"I'm afraid I agree with you, love. Far too many people have been injured and maimed already," Tom said, with a depth of sincerity that was almost prophetic. "Too many people's lives have been shattered by the careless use of fireworks. Some people still haven't got the message that fireworks are dangerous."

Claire agreed emphatically, a frown crossing her pretty face, "I think we should have a ban on it."

Jimmy pulled a face at this remark, "Ooh! Just listen to Claire," he mocked pulling a face at her, "but I bet you'll be there tonight, watching the firework display."

"Yes! I will!" said a defensive Claire. "But, for your information.... Jimmy Lucas, tonight's firework display happens to be organised by the Parent/Teachers Association, and besides," she said in an attempt to put Jimmy in his place, "they have ropes around to keep everyone at a safe distance."

Jimmy folded his arms and pulled another face, "Ooh! Boring!"

Claire turned to Tom, "I should make sure Bella is safely indoors tonight, Tom, animals don't like fireworks." She stroked Bella's head as she spoke.

Bella had tired of the children fussing her and now sat with her head on Tom's knee. "Don't worry love, I don't like fireworks either, so I'll be sure to get Bella home in plenty of time before they start letting them off."

"That's good," said Claire and a smile chased the frown from her face.

"I saw your photo in the paper again last week, Tom," said David. "Bella must be the most famous guide dog for miles around."

There was a great deal of pride in Tom's voice as he spoke softly, "Yes! I think she is.... she must be the only dog with a full diary of engagements."

Rosie came running across the grass and flung her arms around Bella. "Here's Rosie coming to see Bella," said Claire.

"Coming to see David, you mean," said Jimmy, with his quick wit. David grabbed hold of Jimmy and playfully twisted the laughing Jimmy's ear.

"Ignore those two, Tom," said an impatient Claire. She could never understand why boys had to resort to such behaviour.

Rosie flung her arms around Bella, "Who's a gorgeous girl then?" she asked as she hugged Bella. Conversation was halted for the moment while Rosie made a fuss of Bella and said 'hello' to Tom.

Jimmy knew he was pushing his luck but he just couldn't resist saying to his friend, "I bet you wish you were Bella, don't you?"

David glared at Jimmy with eyes that dared him to say another word. Jimmy got the message and started looking for his track suit among the clothes that now lay strewn around the seat. David joined him. It was getting quite cold now.

"Rosie, Tom was just telling us that Bella's got a full diary of engagements, " said Claire, bringing her friend up to date. "What sort of engagements does Bella have, Tom?"

"Well now," Tom was happy to explain. "For instance, next week she will be making a public appearance at a charity concert, opening new shop in the precinct off Kimberley Street, and... oh yes, giving a speech at a school."

Jimmy, now zipping up his track suit, couldn't resist this one. "You mean, Bella talks as well!" he exclaimed.

"No!" laughed Tom, "I do the talking and Bella just sits there and flashes those big brown eyes of hers."

David, looking puzzled, asked "How do you find time to do all those things?"

Tom cleared his throat and said, "There's an old saying Where there's a will, there's a way. And then, of course, there are the three Ds. Do any of you know what they stand for?"

The children looked at each other before confirming that they didn't know.

"Well now," said Tom raising a finger, "the first D is for Desire. In other words you must want to do whatever it is. Secondly," he said as he raised another finger, "D stands for Determination," he paused for a moment before saying, "Nothing is impossible if you have determination, no mountain too high to climb and there is no dream that cannot come true, if only you have the determination to make it so." Raising a third finger, Tom said, "The third D is for Do. Do is a small word that has great meaning. Too many people say, 'I would like to do this, or be that. They think about it but never actually DO anything about it; such people are called dreamers. But those that have the Desire and Determination to Do something about it, can actually make their dreams come true."

Tom encouraged the children to repeat the three Ds aloud, so that they remembered them more easily. "Well done!" said Tom satisfied with their performance. He felt somehow that he could reach children; that he was on their wavelength: he'd often wished he could have been a teacher.

Jimmy jumped up from the games bag he had been sitting on, rubbing his hands in anticipation, as he asked Tom if Bella could have a game of ball with them. Jimmy could see that their games master was still busy with another group of boys.

Claire asked with a slight hesitation, "She is allowed…. isn't she?"

"Yes! She's allowed a free run," Tom assured her. He put his hand down to reach for Bella's harness and hearing the words "Free run" she was immediately on her feet and pushing her cold nose into David's pocket.

"Go and see Jimmy," laughed David, and the black Labrador looked across at Jimmy. She could hardly contain herself as Tom struggled to unhook the white harness. Finally, he lifted the harness off and patted her on the rump, saying, "There you go, Bella."

Excited, Bella made a dash for Jimmy who was enticing her with a large ball. The others soon joined in, leaving Tom on his own, but he didn't mind for he knew Bella needed a free run now and again; it was good for her to have a charge around and it was natural for her to let off steam in this way now and again.

Jimmy threw the ball to David who shouted, "Come on then, Bella, come and get it." Bella jumped for the ball in

mid-air as David threw it to Rosie, but Rosie missed it. Claire was now in possession of the ball and called, "Come on Bella.... Catch it," and she did.

At first she found it difficult to hold in her soft mouth but eventually she managed it and dashed off with the children in pursuit. Jimmy testing his Rugby skills went in for a tackle and grabbed her playfully, rolling on the ground before easing the ball from her mouth. "Got you!" he shouted, and the gentle natured Labrador offered no resistance.

Jimmy, with the ball now in his hands, called across to David, "Let's have a game of football, shall we?"

"All right," replied his friend, who looked across at his sister saying, "Claire can be goalie." He braced himself for her reaction.

"I'm not being goalie," shouted Claire indignantly. "You boys are far too rough, you aim the ball at me instead of the goal."

Rosie saved the day. "I'll be in goal if you like."

David was impressed and said, "Well done! Rosie!" as he placed two anoraks on the grass to represent goal posts.

They all joined in the game, including Bella, who began to get a bit exasperated as she dashed back and forth trying to snatch the ball.

Suddenly Jimmy placed a beautiful shot, high in the air, over Rosie's head right between their make-shift goal posts and onto the far side of the playing field. One of the boys with Mr Mason thought he was being helpful by intercepting the ball and managed to kick it even further away.

Bella was well ahead of the children; one thing she was good at and that was running fast. The ball had disappeared over the hedge towards the swing park area. Bella was ahead and dashed through the shrubbery into the swing park, making her momentarily invisible to the children.

Suddenly, there was a loud, deafening, BANG!.... a sound that relayed echoes all round the park. David and

Jimmy ahead of the others stopped in their tracks. "What was that?" shouted David.

"I don't know" replied a worried Jimmy, "but we'd better find out.... Quick!" The four of them raced across to the swings, not quite knowing what to expect.

"There it is," shouted Jimmy, as a firework still smouldered on the path by one of the swings.

Claire panicked, "Bella!", she shouted. "Where is Bella?"

Rosie put her hand to her mouth as she realised what had happened.

"There she is!" shouted Jimmy, catching sight of a terrified Bella racing across the park and into the distance. "Bella! Come back!" he shouted as he ran after her, followed by the others.

David suddenly stopped. "Wait!" he called out, and the others slowed down and stopped, trying to catch their breath.

"We can't leave the park without Mr Mason's permission." He spun round. "Come on, we'd better do this properly."

Jimmy was still breathless, but agreed, along with the girls. "All right!" he said, "but we'd better hurry or Bella will be miles away."

Bursting through the children grouped around Mr Mason, David gasped, "Please, Sir! Someone threw a banger in the swing park and Bella's bolted. We thought we had better get permission to go and look for her."

"Yes! Yes! Off you go!" said the games teacher with a wave of his hand. He had a sinking feeling at the very thought of what might happen if Bella were not found. He decided that himself and the children in his charge would search in the opposite direction to the others and briefed the children on safety before setting off, when he suddenly realised that poor Tom was sat all alone.

"Just a minute," he said halting the eager children, "Someone ought to stay with Tom.... Melanie, will you?"

"Yes Sir!" came the willing reply from the petite girl with long hair, who hoped to be a ballet dancer.

Tom shivered against the cold damp air, as his senses told him all was not well. He too had heard the 'Bang!' followed by the commotion and felt a certain sense of relief when he heard Melanie's footsteps running towards him.

"Hello! Tom. It's me, Melanie!"

Tom held out his hand. "Where's…. Bella?" he asked, half-afraid to hear the answer. Melanie took his hand and then sat beside him on the seat.

"Don't worry," she said, in the hope of reassuring the blind man. It was some stupid boy who let off a banger in the swing park, and frightened Bella, but…." She felt Tom tense up. "She can't have gone far. David, Jimmy, Rosie and Claire have gone off to look for her and Mr Mason is searching the other playing fields area with the rest of the children. "Don't worry, Tom, they will find Bella…. you'll see."

Tom felt his heart sink. He tried to think rationally and told himself - "Of course, Bella would come back, she had just gone around the park, and Bella knows the park better than most. She will be back." Suddenly an inner fear crept over him, a fear he had never allowed to surface before…. What if Bella was lost…. What if she was killed on the road? "No!" he agonised, he couldn't bear to think about life without Bella.

"Don't worry, Tom," said Melanie gently placing her hand on his. "They will find her for you."

How Tom wished he had Melanie's confidence. "I hope so," he sighed and paused for a moment while his unseeing eyes scanned the dark world out there in front of him. Melanie saw his eyes mist over as he spoke, "Dear God! I hope so!" His voice trailed off into a whispered tear, and the park felt so empty, so quiet, so…. alien.

CHAPTER FIVE: THE BALLOON GOES UP

All hope of finding Bella still in the park began to fade for David and his friends as they stopped for a breather. "Where on earth can she have got to?" said Rosie, puffing and tugging at her track suit to let some cool air circulate around her body.

Jimmy had lost some of his wit and appeared very worried, "I don't know!" he said, as they all sat exhausted on a park bench. "But if I hadn't asked Tom to let Bella off her harness for a run, none of this would have happened."

David felt sorry for his friend, "Come on, Jimmy!" he said, "it's not your fault. It's the idiot who threw that banger."

Jimmy looked out across the park and then kicked at a loose stone with the toe of his trainer. "Just wait 'til I catch him."

He felt a little better knowing David was on his side, and the two girls were just as sympathetic.

However, Claire was more concerned about finding Bella. "Poor Bella!" she said. "I wonder where she can be?"

Rosie spotted a woman coming towards them, a shopping basket on her arm, "Let's ask if she's seen a black Labrador."

David took the initiative, asking if she had seen a dog, and giving Bella's description.

"Now wait a minute, dear," she said thoughtfully, "I did see a black dog over by the pond.... with two small children and their mother."

"Oh great!" said David with an immense feeling of relief, "That sounds like Bella." Jimmy, Claire and Rosie were up ready for action. Jimmy gave his friend the 'thumbs up' sign as they offered their thanks. But before they had run more than a few yards, she called, "Just a minute. I've just remembered. The dog I saw had a white patch over its eye... is that the one?"

"Oh No!" called back David, who felt as though he had

had all the wind knocked out of him, "But thanks anyway." She wished them luck in their search and went on her way.

Jimmy couldn't hide his disappointment. "I bet she doesn't know a Labrador from a sheep dog." His remark brought a touch of humour to the situation and they laughed briefly.

Rosie, hands on her hips, scanning the perimeter of the park suddenly had an idea. "I've just thought," she said, "Bella might have headed for the woods at the back of the playing fields."

David agreed with her. "You might be right, Rosie," he said, "but I think we should get back to Mr Mason and organise a proper search party."

"What about lunch?" asked Jimmy in a plaintive voice.

Claire found his remark most irritating. "How can you even think of food at a time like this?" she said with a pout. Jimmy was just about to give her a short swift answer, when David intervened.

"Come on, you two, we can't waste time arguing."

Melanie was still sitting with Tom when Mr Mason and his group of children arrived back from their search. David reported that they had had no luck either. Mr Mason sighed, "We've covered the whole park between us and there's no sign of her."

Rosie offered her suggestion that Bella might have headed for the woods. Mr Mason agreed that there was a strong possibility. He looked down at the sad figure of Tom.

"Tom!" said an anxious Mr Mason, "I think what we should do is get you home safely before we organise a proper search party." He tried to give Tom a ray of hope. "Who knows," he said, "Bella might be there already, waiting for you."

"Please God," said Tom almost praying, "Let her be there."

Mr Mason put a kindly hand on Tom's shoulder, "Don't worry, Tom, we'll find her for you."

David and Jimmy took Tom safely home, but unfortunately there was no Bella. In the meantime, Mr Mason took the rest of the children back to school for a late lunch, saving some for David and Jimmy.

During lunch, with the Head's blessing, Mr Mason enlisted the help of two teachers who had a free period, to help organise the children into a search party. It was two thirty when the search party arrived at the clearing in the woods. The teachers were all too well aware that time was of the essence, as it would begin to get dark around four thirty and, if they hadn't found Bella by then, they would have no alternative but to inform the police of Bella's disappearance.

Once Mr Mason had checked that everyone was present, he split them into three groups with a teacher in charge of each group; one group to search to the right of the woods, another to search the left of the woods, leaving himself and his group the centre section. "Have you all got that?" he shouted, and a volley of affirmatives came back. "Then we'll all meet up here in this clearing when we have completed the search.... Good Luck!" he said as he ushered each group off to search for the missing guide dog. David and his sister, Claire, along with Rosie and Jimmy, had been assigned to Mr Mason's group.

David was the first to arrive back in the clearing ahead of his group and dropped down exhausted onto a fallen tree trunk. He sat forward with his head in his hands, saying "Oh Bella! Where are you?" It was beginning to get dark; David felt an uneasy silence in the clearing and found himself wishing the others would hurry up. Suddenly a noisy rustling through the bushes startled him. "Oh! It's you Rosie," he said with relief. "Any luck?"

Rosie almost threw herself onto the log beside David. "No!" she said wearily. There's no sign of her anywhere and I'm worn out."

David kicked absent-mindedly at the leaves on the

ground. "Do you know?" he said, looking into the distant woodland, "between us we have covered these entire woods and come up with nothing." He paused to make a circle in the leaves with his foot. "A big fat zero." David felt tears prick the back of his eyes and turned his head away.

Rosie was just as disheartened, "I know," she said, running her fingers through her hair, "but Bella must be somewhere." She sat silently for a moment then turned her head away as her eyes filled with tears. "Oh David!" she cried softly, "what if Bella is lying injured somewhere...." she could hardly bear to think of it, "....or dead?" she sobbed into her hands.

David felt awkward trying to comfort Rosie, though he hated to see her upset. He put his arm around her shoulder, "Don't cry Rosie, we'll find Bella soon," he said in a wavering voice, "it's just a matter of time.... that's all."

Rosie sniffled and tried to wipe her tears with the back of her hand.

"Here!" offered David, fishing a neatly folded white handkerchief out of his tracksuit pocket, "I've only used it once, honest" he said laughing, in an attempt to lighten the atmosphere.

Rosie wiped away her tears and smiled. "You know, David, you have a way of making things seem all right. I always feel much better when I'm with you," she finished in a rush.

David felt himself blushing. "That's good, Rosie," was all he could say. For months he had cherished a secret dream that Rosie would feel the same about him as he felt about her. In his eyes she was a princess, the most beautiful girl in the world. He was just wondering whether to chance a kiss when there was a sudden rustle of leaves at the edge of the clearing.

David's arm shot swiftly back to his side. "Shhhhh!" he said in a low voice, "I can hear voices."

Rosie listened for a minute, "It's only Jimmy and Claire.

I left them collecting leaves for their scrapbook, and the rest of the group can't be far behind."

David pulled a face and sighed, "I suppose we'll be in trouble for splitting up from the group."

Just then Jimmy and Claire came into sight. "Phew!" said Jimmy, "I feel as though I've walked fifty miles," as he stopped on the edge of the clearing. Even a fifty-mile walk could not suppress his sense of humour. "Hello?" he teased, "What are you two doing alone in the woods, may I ask?"

David was quick off the mark, "The same as you, clever clogs," he said huffily. "We've just been having a rest, that's all."

Jimmy smiled from ear to ear. "A likely story!" he laughed.

David glared at him. The kind of glare that always told the jovial Jimmy that he'd said enough. As Jimmy and Claire joined them on the tree trunk, Rosie asked where the rest of the group were. Claire confirmed that they were on their way.

"Well, no one has found Bella, so she can't be anywhere in these woods," said Jimmy. Claire asked worriedly, "What are we going to do?" She hoped one of them might come up with an answer. She sat wringing her hands nervously as she thought of poor Tom.

Suddenly David jumped up from the log and threw his hands in the air, "What do we always do?" he asked, looking at three rather blank faces, "We don't panic! That's what we do." Rosie smiled, impressed at the way David had of phrasing his sentences; to make you think. "Now!" he said taking command of the situation, "I think we're going to have to take this a stage further and approach the various authorities." He paused for a moment biting his bottom lip. "Perhaps we should draw up a list of people to contact.... like the police, schools, bus stations and the railway station."

"I could call at the police station on my way home," offered Jimmy enthusiastically. David had managed to get their brains into gear.

Rosie jumped up from the tree trunk, "What about the taxi drivers?" she asked eagerly, "They could look out for Bella."

David agreed with her. "Why not?" he said, picking up a stick from the ground.

Claire shouted with her own brand of enthusiasm, "We could put 'LOST DOG' cards in all the shop windows..... especially the pet shops." Her mind was racing along now, "I could even ring the Guide Dog Centre at Barrington," she said excitedly.

Jimmy immediately dashed her enthusiasm by saying, "Don't be silly Claire, that's miles away and besides Bella won't go more than ten miles away, that's how she has been trained."

Claire refused to be completely deflated by the likes of Jimmy Lucas. "Well, I still think it's worth a phone call," she said as she pulled a face at Jimmy.

"Hey!" said Rosie thoughtfully, "I've just had a thought."

"Careful!" came Jimmy's bantering voice, "thinking can be bad for you."

Rosie was far too clever to fall for Jimmy's bait and turned to the others before continuing, "I could get in touch with the RSPCA, the dog clubs and local kennels.... just in case someone finds Bella and takes her to one of them."

"Good idea!" said David. His mind was working overtime now. The others would be joining them soon and he wanted to have some constructive ideas to put forward to Mr Mason. He also used the logic that the games teacher might not be quite so cross with them for splitting up from their group if he could show that they had utilised their time. He clicked his fingers as an idea came to him, "Listen!" he said, placing a foot up on the fallen tree trunk where the other three now sat. "I have an idea..We could call into the local Evening Chronicle office and get them to print a front page story about Bella's disappearance." They all agreed it was a brilliant idea. David had another thought, "I suppose they will need a photograph of Bella, though."

Jimmy squeaked, in a voice that sounded a full octave higher than normal.... "A PHOTOGRAPH OF BELLA....!" He took a breath, "They should have a whole album full.... The number they have taken in the past few months."

David smiled, "Yes! Of course! You're right Jimmy."

Claire felt slightly irritated as she saw Jimmy 'chalk one up' to himself, but she had regained her enthusiasm. "I hope they'll print the story in all the newspapers, then it will reach every farmhouse and village in the county. They were very dejected however when David pointed out that it was obviously too late for today's papers.

Suddenly there was a burst of action from David that made them all jump. He took his foot off the tree trunk, slapped his fist into his hand and shouted, "I've had a brainwave."

"Is it contagious," asked a giggling Jimmy.

"Now don't fool around Jimmy, this is no time for jokes," David warned. "Listen!" he said. "What's the quickest and most efficient way of getting a message across to Joe Public?"

"Radio!" shouted Jimmy.

"Yes!" David confirmed but emphasised, "Local Radio!"

"Hey!" That's a brilliant idea," agreed Jimmy. Rosie and Claire nodded.

"We'll get in touch with Radio Westfield and ask them to put out a description of Bella over the air," David said and added, "I might even ask them if I could make a personal appeal over the air..that would have more effect."

"Brilliant!" said Rosie, "Can we come too?" David agreed but wondered whether the radio station would allow them all into the studio.

They heard voices from the wood as the others approached the clearing. "Sounds like our group," he said sitting down on the tree trunk. The others joined him.

The remainder of the search party returned to the clearing and Mr Mason noticed the four sitting completely rested upon the tree trunk. "Why aren't you with your group?" he asked in an ominous tone of voice.

"I'm sorry, Sir!" said David accepting full responsibility, "We took the wrong turning, which split us up from our group." Mr Mason sighed heavily and as David saw the frown appear on his face, he quickly added. "I....er, I took full responsibility for our splinter group, Sir, and we continued searching for Bella." Mr Mason could not help but admire David's leadership qualities in a boy of his age. David continued to explain, "And as you said we should all meet back in the clearing, I didn't see the need to panic, Sir."

Mr Mason sighed again, "All right, I'll let you off this time. But....," he glared at the group, "the next time you are told to stay with your group, you will do just that.... do you understand?"

A grateful Jimmy, David, Rosie and Claire, nodded sheepishly, and in unison answered, "Yes, Sir!" Mr Mason then advised the rest of the search party to take a rest - that is, those that had not flopped down with sheer exhaustion already.

The light which had earlier filtered through the trees into the clearing was now fading fast and mist shrouded the trees increasing the nip in the air.

Mr Mason's voice held a note of disappointment as he addressed the children around him. "Well, there's no sign of Bella here," he said, noting the look of defeat in the children's faces as he explained that the 'balloon would now have to go up'; the other teachers agreed with him.

Then David raised his hand in the air, "Sir!" he said eagerly, "We've been discussing what we should do next." He looked at Jimmy, Rosie and Claire, hoping that they would back him up.

"Oh yes?" said the games teacher, folding his arms and waiting for David to continue.

David plucked up courage, "Between us," he said, "we've decided we should contact the police, RSPCA, bus crews, taxi drivers, and.... oh," he said almost forgetting, "The Evening Chronicle, Sir."

Mr Mason looked impressed. "Well done!" he said, encouraging David to continue.

"We could try to get them to print a front page story... all about Bella's disappearance."

Jimmy couldn't resist adding "That's, of course, if Bella doesn't turn up before."

Rosie couldn't miss this opportunity of praising David in front of the others. "David has even thought of contacting the local radio station to see if they will put out a description of Bella, and possibly making a personal appeal himself."

David smiled, feeling just a hint of embarrassment, "Well, Sir", he said, "it's one way of reaching every home in the county."

Everyone thought it was an excellent idea. Mr Mason said that there was a Parent Teachers Association meeting the following evening and he would also spread the word there.

Basher, who was intrigued by David's plans put up his hand excitedly, "Sir?" he said, thinking this was his big chance. "What about CB Radio? My Dad's a long-distance lorry driver and he could put a message over the air on his CB rig." Little Tim McCreadie, who was sat at his friend's side, nudged Basher's elbow and giggled at this suggestion, but Basher was not going to let it spoil his moment. "I could ask him to send out a message to all the other CB users, Sir, asking them to look out for Bella."

Mr Mason paused as he considered the idea, "Hmm!" he frowned, "CB users can be a confounded nuisance at times. But... there again," he said, "they have been known to come up trumps at a time like this." He stroked his beard, "All right, Basher," he agreed, "you can ask your Dad to send out an 'earball'... or whatever the jargon is."

There was a sudden burst of muted laughter through which Basher tried to correct the games teacher. "I think you mean an 'eyeball', Sir."

"Yes! Yes!" said the embarrassed Mr Mason, "Whatever they call it... it might just work."

Silence reigned once more as the group ran out of inspirations, Claire was getting more and more anxious. "Where can Bella have got to?" she said nervously.

Melanie was the first to answer. "I don't know," she said, "but she must be getting pretty hungry."

Little Tim, who had noted the ebbing light, said, "It will be dark soon."

Basher added, "Yeah! and it's bonfire night too." he said adding, "Just think of all those rockets and bangers.... she'll be scared stiff."

Rosie sighed at the very thought, "Poor Bella," she said tearfully, "we'll have to find her soon."

Claire looked up at the swirling mist around the tree tops and shivered. "If Bella isn't found by midnight, she said wringing her hands as she often did when she was worried or anxious, "she's going to be cold, hungry and tired. But.... where's she going to sleep?"

"Well!" said Mr Mason in an attempt to lift the mood, "let's hope we find her before then." He looked at his watch, "It's nearly half-past-four.... I think we ought to call it a day or you'll all be too tired for the fireworks tonight." He noticed a distinct apathy from the children in front of him at the mention of the word "fireworks".

Mr Mason addressed the search party in a more formal manner. "I suggest we get back to school as it will be completely dark soon, and if we have heard no news of Bella at five o'clock then I'm afraid" he said looking at David and his friends, "we'll have no choice but to follow through with the plans we have made this afternoon." David nodded in agreement as the games teacher turned towards his two colleagues. "We had better get them safely back to school," he said half jokingly, "before they send out a search party for us."

CHAPTER SIX: HAVE YOU SEEN BELLA?

The pungent smell of smouldering wood was all that remained of Bonfire Night, but there was still no sign of Bella. The morning air was shrouded in a depressive mist that seemed to herald the start of winter. Bella had been missing for almost twenty-four hours now, but to her blind owner it seemed like a lifetime. One of the biggest searches of its kind had now been launched to find the missing guide dog. Tom sat alone, waiting and praying - as he had done all through the night - that she would come home.

Tom sat hugging Bella's harness, feeling helplessly alone. The untouched bowl of water by the kitchen door had meant a night of heartbreak for him. He rocked to and fro in his chair, as if the motion somehow helped to soothe his troubled mind. "Oh Bella!" he cried to himself, "Where are you?" He had never felt more alone and helpless as he did right now.

An urgent ring on the door bell made him start. He jumped up from his chair, it might be news of Bella he thought and felt his way to the front door as quickly as he could.

As Tom opened the door a voice said, "Hello! Mr Sinclair. It's me, Mike Bretton, from the Evening Chronicle."

"Oh... oh, hello." Although he recognised Mike's voice, Tom sounded somewhat vague. "Won't you come in?" he said, almost mechanically.

"Not a very nice day," said Mike as he followed Tom into the living room, not relishing the thought of this interview.

"Please sit down," said Tom automatically. Mike made himself comfortable in a chair before proceeding.

"I... er, I believe you've lost Bella?" The friendly reporter tried to make his voice as sympathetic as possible.

Tom took a deep breath and braced himself for the interview knowing it was to be his toughest. "Yes!" he said sadly, "I'm afraid so."

"A young man, by the name of David Jeffries, came into

our office to ask if we could run a front page story about Bella's disappearance and told us what had happened." Mike's job as a reporter brought him into contact with many sad cases and he had learned to channel the emotions in such cases.

Tom's pale gaunt face managed a brief smile. "Yes! That's the sort of thing David would do."

"Mr Sinclair.... " Mike hesitated, "Tom, I know this must be very painful for you, but have you any idea at all where Bella might be?" Tom sank back into his chair and shook his head slowly.

"No!" Tom spoke with a heavy heart. "The only thing I do know is, I haven't had a wink of sleep since she went missing." He tried to compose himself. "It.... feels as if a light has gone out of my life," he said, holding back the tears.

It was Mike Bretton who felt helpless now. "Oh, I'm sure she will turn up soon, Mr Sinclair," he said, trying to muster some enthusiasm.

"I wish I could believe that," said Tom, nervously rubbing his hands together. "But Bella's never gone missing before. In all the years we've been together, she has never left my side." He bit on his trembling lip, "If anything has happened to her," he sobbed, "I don't know what I'll do." Suddenly, the tears flowed unashamedly.

Mike didn't say a word. There is a time for talking and time for keeping quiet. Tom fumbled for his handkerchief and wiped his eyes. "Bella...." he sniffed, "was everything beautiful in my life - she was my best friend, my companion, my eyes...." he sobbed. "She was my whole life."

It was not easy, even for a seasoned reporter like Mike Bretton, to sit and remain untouched by the ultimate love and devotion a blind man and his dog felt for each other. "Perhaps someone has taken her into their home, not knowing she is a guide dog," suggested Mike, trying to give Tom some hope.

But then Tom's tears turned to anger. "If anyone is

holding Bella against her will," he said rapping his knuckles on the arm of his chair, "they will have me to answer to." His face was tense and drained of all colour. "No!" he said shaking his head automatically, "I won't give up until I find her." He turned in the direction of Mike, who was writing his notes. "You can put this in your paper," he said with new found determination, "I'm willing to offer fifty pounds...." he paused, "No! make that one hundred pounds reward to anyone who can find Bella, or anyone who can give me information leading to Bella's safe return."

"That's a very generous reward," said Mike as he wrote it down in his notes.

"It will be worth every penny to have Bella back home with me..where she belongs," said Tom, settling back in his chair. "I promise," he said, "I won't leave a single stone unturned until I find her." He banged on his chair with his hand to stress his determination. "I'll search to the ends of the earth if I have to." The interview was suddenly interrupted by a ring on the door bell. "Will you excuse me for a moment," asked Tom as he made his way into the hall. Mike was just putting the final notes to the story when he thought he recognised the voice of the caller at the front door.

"Hello! Tom. It's David and Jimmy." David shivered in the cold November air. "We've come to see how you are."

Tom assured the two boys that he was coping as he ushered them into the living room. "Er.... this is Mike Bretton from the Evening Chronicle," said Tom in an effort to be polite.

"We've already met," said Mike with a smile.

"Oh yes," said Tom, "of course, do forgive me. Come nearer to the fire boys and get yourselves warm."

Tom settled back into his chair, half afraid to ask the question which he knew he must. "Is there still no news of Bella?" he asked softly.

"No!" said David as he leaned towards the fire to warm

his hands, "I'm afraid not." His handsome young features full of compassion for the saddened blind man. "We've had half the school out looking for Bella," sighed David. "We've contacted the police, taxi drivers, bus crews, dog clubs, dog kennels, RSPCA, the Guide Dogs for the Blind Association, pet shops and...." he drew a deep breath, "we've even been in touch with the local radio station, who are going to let us make a personal appeal!"

Jimmy piped in, "Live - this afternoon!"

David suddenly had a thought. "Tom?" he asked, then paused, "How would you like to come with us... and then perhaps you could make the appeal."

Tom was taken slightly aback, he hadn't thought of making an appeal himself.

"Yes!" said an excited Jimmy, "that would have more effect." Tom seemed a little apprehensive about the idea. "That is, if you feel up to it," concluded Jimmy.

Tom sat up straight in his chair. He knew his positive thinking had to start right away. "Yes!" he said with confidence. "Yes! I will. If it means getting Bella back.... I certainly will." He started to straighten his shirt and his tie. "What time do we have to be there?" he asked with a renewed air of confidence.

"Not until two o'clock," said David. "We have plenty of time....don't worry."

Jimmy looked over at Mike who was finalising his notes. "Are you going to put it on the front page Mr Bretton?" he asked hopefully.

The reporter shook his head slowly and tut-tutted. "I don't know about that," he said, not wanting to promise the boys too much, "I'll have to ask my editor. We might be able to squeeze it in."

Jimmy's voice reached an all time high on the scale as he shrieked, "Squeeze it in!" His face went bright pink. "We were hoping you would fill it out in large.... bold.... print," saying - with a dramatic wave of his arm in mid air he mimicked the headlines - "BELLA MISSING! The search is on for the famous guide dog Bella who went missing on..."

Mike interrupted the budding journalist. "Oh! Very good!" he said with a sardonic smile, "We could do with you on the paper."

David laughed as Jimmy looked pleadingly at the reporter, with eyes that almost willed him into submission. David suddenly looked more serious, "But... Mr Bretton," he said carefully, not wishing to lose any ground, "Bella has given you lots of news stories for your paper in the past, so..." he pleaded, "couldn't you do this for her?"

Mike scratched his head with his pen. "I suppose you do have a point," he said, then his face brightened. "All right!" he agreed. "It goes out on the front page," and looking hard at Jimmy he emphasised, "In Bold Print!"

"Great!" the two boys shouted in unison.

Tom smiled at their determination.

Jimmy, however, still wasn't satisfied. "How about the Nationals," he asked excitedly. "Can't we get it in those too?"

Mike Bretton smiled and shook his head at the same time, "My goodness... you do drive a hard bargain, don't you?" he said, but he had to admire the young man's tenacity. "All right!" he said, "I'll see what I can do." He saw Jimmy wink at David and was quick to add, "But.... don't expect it to be on the front page of the nationals, will you?"

Jimmy's smile was one of victory. "Thanks! Mr Bretton," he beamed.

"Well, I must be off now, Mr Sinclair," said Mike, putting his notebook and pen into his pocket, and swinging his woollen scarf around his neck, "If I'm going to get this in today's edition. Thanks for talking to me." The reporter looked at the expression on Tom's face. "Let's hope we get a positive response to the story."

Tom, managing a half-smile, said, "Yes! I certainly hope so." Mike offered to see himself out and Tom thanked him for coming.

The two boys also thanked Mike, and just as he was

about to disappear through the living room door, Jimmy called after him.

"Don't forget, Mr Bretton," he winked, "if you need any help, I'm available."

Mike couldn't hide his smile as he replied, "Yes! I'll remember."

Tom heard the front door close which told him that the reporter was on his way to get the story into print. The thought pleased him, and yet... it frightened him. Pushing it to the back of his mind for the moment, he enquired, "Where are the two girls? They are usually with you, aren't they?"

David smiled at Tom, "Oh! they're getting ready to go to the radio station."

Jimmy raised his eyes to the ceiling and tut-tutted. "Girls!" he exclaimed, "Anyone would think they were going to be seen on the radio."

David was quick to defend them while Tom smiled softly, "You know what girls are like," he said nonchalantly addressing Tom, "they like to look their best." Tom agreed. David glanced at his wristwatch and saw that it was already eleven o'clock. "We had also better be going now, Tom, but we'll call for you at about one-fifteen.... if that's OK with you?"

Tom agreed and enquired how they were all going to get there. David reassured him by saying, "My mother has an estate car, so we'll all be able to get in." David looked hard at Jimmy, daring him to complain as he continued, "Jimmy and I can always squeeze in the back if necessary."

Tom sounded relieved. "That's good," he said, "I was worried for a moment."

The two boys zipped up their anoraks ready to leave. "Are you sure you'll be all right, Tom?" asked Jimmy.

"Yes" said Tom, "I'll be fine.... don't worry about me."

David saw a glimpse of sadness cross Tom's face and endeavoured to reassure him. "We'll have Bella back with you in no time at all, Tom," said David, in an attempt to inspire faith to keep their blind friend company and give him some hope to hold on to. "We won't give up until we find her for you."

Tom was touched by their kindness and felt their sheer determination lift his spirits. At the front door he thanked his two young friends and promised to be ready at one-fifteen. As he closed the front door again, the telephone rang; it was the first of a whole series of calls with offers of help.

* * * * *

Mrs Jeffries had just finished clearing away after lunch when David breezed into the kitchen. "Are you ready, Mum?" he enquired, looking anxiously at his watch. "It's almost five to-one."

"Yes dear!" said his mother, taking off her apron and automatically hanging it on the back of the kitchen door. "I just have to freshen up, I won't be a moment," she called as she ran up the stairs.

David stood in the hallway at the bottom of the stairs looking irritated as he waited for his mother to come downstairs again. "What's Claire doing?" he asked with a sigh as she descended the stairs.

"She's still in her room getting ready," said his mother as she clutched her open handbag, checking to see that she had her keys, cheque-book, purse, lipstick and a handkerchief; the latter she was going to need more than she realised.

David drummed his fingers on the stair-rail as he shouted up the stairs at the top of his voice, "Claire! Aren't you ready yet?"

"Yes!" shouted back Claire, annoyed that her brother was rushing her, "I'm coming!"

They collected Tom from his home and then picked up Jimmy and Rosie at a pre-arranged point outside the school gates and arrived at the Radio Westfield studios at ten minutes to two.

At the reception desk Mrs Jeffries explained who they were and why they were there. The receptionist suggested they have a seat. Marion Jeffries, Tom, Rosie and Claire did so, but David and Jimmy preferred to look around.

Jimmy was fascinated by the wall of glass which separated each of the occupied studios. As he wondered which one they would be in he turned to David saying tentatively, "I think I'll be a disc jockey when I leave school," as he continued to peer through the glass wall. Mrs Jeffries saw the receptionist smile and wondered how many impressionable young boys she had heard say the same thing.

Claire was intrigued by the hidden speakers in the ceiling of the reception area that were relaying the transmission going out to millions of homes in the region.

Tom sat quietly ringing his hands as he heard the receptionist relay a message to Studio Three, in connection with their arrival. Tom felt his stomach churn at the very thought of talking on radio.

Chris Mallen was busy preparing for the news spot in Studio Three. Dave Bembow, the DJ, in trendy gear, was winding down his two-hour spot of popular music and placed a long playing disc on the turntable while he went out to reception. Marion thought he looked years younger than he sounded over the air as he crossed the reception area to speak with the girl at the desk.

Approaching the waiting group he said cheerfully, "Hello! I believe you are here to make an appeal for the missing guide dog, Bella." He looked at Tom saying, "And you must be Mr Sinclair... Bella's owner."

"Yes!" said Tom nervously, "I am."

The DJ smiled understandingly, "We feel we know you and Bella, Mr Sinclair. We've covered many news items about you and I'm very pleased to meet you." Tom smiled and offered the DJ his hand. Tom then briefly introduced Marion Jeffries and all his young friends.

The DJ then looked round the group and scratched his head thoughtfully. "Would it be possible," he asked, not wishing to upset anyone, "if just one of you accompanied

Mr Sinclair to the studio." He went on to explain, "There's not a great deal of room in the studios at the best of times."

Everyone's eyes turned to David, who was the obvious choice. "All right!" he agreed "I'll go with Tom." He felt proud that he had been unanimously voted for the task.

"Right!" said the DJ, with an ear listening to his music. "Perhaps you'd like to follow me?" He was good at his job and knew that the ultimate crime for any DJ was to have a pregnant pause filling the airways at the end of a disc. He knew, as did his colleagues, that only in a life or death situation was that ever permissible.

Dave offered Tom his arm and they went through to Studio Three where they were introduced to Chris Mallen. Chris helped Tom to relax a little with a brief description of the procedure. They then exchanged a few words in preparation for the appeal. David was fascinated by all the knobs and buttons on the control desk in each studio, not to mention the agility with which the presenters used them.

Two minutes seemed like two hours as Tom tried to gather his nervous thoughts into some kind of order.

Marion Jeffries and the children had wished him luck and he knew he was going to need it. He wanted desperately to make a success of the appeal, but he was afraid of making a hash of the whole thing by fluffing his carefully chosen words.... the ones he had gone over and over during the car journey to Radio Westfield.

Then Tom heard the DJ saying, "Well folks, that's the end of the Midday Show. But I'll be back with you tomorrow, same time.... same place. So do join me. I'll look forward to having the pleasure of your company. The news will be coming up shortly, read by Chris Mallen in our newsroom."

As the theme tune played the show out and off the air, the adrenalin started to pump around Tom's whole body. In a moment of panic he decided to abandon his carefully memorised words and play the whole thing from his heart. Chris Mallen proceeded to read the national news before reading the local round-up of news. His voice was cool, calm

and precise and Tom wondered how on earth he managed to keep it that way. "And now for the local news."

Tom wished that the ground would open up and swallow him, but he knew in his heart that if there was any chance of finding Bella he had to go through with the appeal.

Chris went straight into Bella's disappearance. He had decided to give the story priority: "One of the biggest searches of its kind has been launched to find missing guide dog, Bella, who ran off after being terrified by a carelessly thrown firework on the afternoon of November the fifth.... Thousands of people throughout the North-West, including bus crews, taxi-drivers, dog clubs and schools have joined in the search to find one of the best-known guide dogs in the country.... Bella recently made the headlines by walking fifty miles with her owner, Mr Tom Sinclair, to celebrate the Guide Dog Association's Golden Jubilee year. Bella is also known to have raised many thousands of pounds for the Guide Dog charity and made more than a thousand public appearances, meeting Royalty and movie stars." He paused a moment to look at Tom who was more than a little nervous. David gripped Tom's arm to let him know that he had his support, as the newscaster continued. "....I have with me in the studio, Bella's owner, Mr Sinclair, who would like to appeal to the public in the hope that someone, somewhere, might have seen his guide dog."

Chris Mallen looked at Tom who was now clenching his hands nervously. "Mr Sinclair, Bella is a very special guide dog isn't she?" He added, "Not just a guide dog, but an Ambassador - if one can use such a word where a guide dog is concerned - for the Guide Dogs for the Blind Association."

Tom tried to make his words audible, "Yes! Yes! She is." He felt that he had to go on to explain, "She has personally been responsible for raising many thousands of pounds for the Guide Dog Association. She has also, as you mentioned Chris, met many famous people, including Royalty."

Chris came in at this point, "And, of course, Bella

became a household name with the coverage of the fifty-mile walk."

Tom managed a half-smile as he added, "And she won many hearts along the way too."

Chris wanting to move the conversation on a little, added, "Quite recently too, I believe she saved your life?"

"Yes!" answered Tom, "She certainly did."

Chris quickly sensed that the memory was too painful for Tom to go into detail about this dreadful incident, and he quickly moved on to the main reason for the blind man's visit to the studios.

"Mr Sinclair?" asked the thoughtful news presenter, "What would you like to say to all those people out there listening now and who might be able to help you?"

Tom braced himself and spoke with calm control, "I would like to say this...."

Marion Jeffries, Claire, Rosie and Jimmy, watched Tom and David through the glass wall, listening intently to every word being relayed over the speakers in the reception area.

Tom cleared his throat and then continued.... "If you see Bella.... or know of her whereabouts, please, please get in touch with me." He was gaining confidence with every sentence now. "Bella is a very friendly and lovable black Labrador. Most of you will have seen her pictures in the newspapers so will know what she looks like. Everyone loves Bella, she has that effect on people. So should you find her.... even though you are bound to find her adorable.... everyone does.... Please, please, send her back to me." There was a note of heartbreak in his voice now as he spoke. "She's not just any dog.... she is my eyes. My.... my whole life!" He paused for a moment to gain control of his feelings, then went on.... "Without Bella," he said movingly, "I am like a leaf in the wind, with no direction." David touched his arm to comfort Tom as he struggled with his emotions and tried to steady his voice. "Without Bella," he said poignantly, "there will be no Christmas for me." He swallowed hard, "and no Happy New Year.... so I beg you," he pleaded with tears in his voice, "Please, please, find Bella for me." His voice trailed off in an audible sob.

Through the glass wall, in the Reception area, Claire looked at Rosie and both girls had tears in their eyes. Marion Jeffries knew she had to be the strong one; she bit her bottom lip, to stop herself from crying. She noticed that even the receptionist had temporarily stopped what she was busy doing and just stood with a misty expression on her face.

Chris Mallen concluded..... "Thank you! Mr Sinclair. Well," he sighed, "I'm sure no one can have failed to have been moved by that appeal." He then gave out the radio station's telephone number so, that in the event of anyone having news of Bella they could telephone Radio Westfield. He finally finished by reading the rest of the local news.

During the car journey back to Seaton, Tom sat in silence trying to remember all he had said over the air, wondering if it had come across all right, even though Marion and his young friends had congratulated him on his excellent appeal. But Tom needn't have worried, Radio Westfield's programme controller had told Chris Mallen, over a cup of tea after the news, that Mr Sinclair's appeal was one of the most moving he had ever heard on radio.

But the question mark hung heavily in all of their minds, "Would they find Bella?"

CHAPTER SEVEN: WHERE DO WE BEGIN?

As Marion Jeffries sipped her cup of hot chocolate, her thoughts were for Tom and how she could help to find his missing guide dog, Bella. David and Claire sat crossed legged either side of the coffee table, half-heartedly playing a game of Scrabble.

It was Claire's turn but she sat with her chin on her hands, unable to think of any word that would make sense and her mind wandered away from the game. "What time is Jimmy supposed to be coming round?" she asked with obvious lack of enthusiasm.

Her brother lifted his eyebrows and sighed, "He said seven o'clock.... but you know Jimmy, he's never on time." He added, hoping his mother wouldn't hear, "I think he must have been born late."

Mrs Jeffries wasn't that deep in her own thoughts and, like all mums, she had a permanent antenna extended where her children were concerned. "David! That's enough now," she scorned.

"But, Mum!" he complained, "You don't know him like I do.... if I had ten pence for every time he's late.... I'd be very rich." At that moment the door bell rang and the clock began striking seven.

Claire teased her brother, "You've just lost ten pence," but David was not in the mood for his sister's jokes.

"Oh shut up Claire," he growled as he stood up to answer the door.

"Now, now, you two, stop squabbling," warned their mother with a frown.

David opened the door to a beaming Jimmy. "To what do we owe this honour, may I ask?" said David, with a hint of sarcasm. Jimmy looked a little confused at David's slightly hostile remark.

"What do you mean?" he asked as they walked through to the sitting room where he said a polite hello to Mrs Jeffries and Claire.

"I mean you being early," said David. He sounded irritated that Jimmy was taking so long to catch on. The jovial Jimmy still had a puzzled expression on his freshly washed face.

"But you said seven o'clock," said Jimmy defensively.

"That's what I mean," said David. However, Jimmy was not going to be like a little fish and bite the bait that his friend was handing out.

He tossed his head with an air of grandeur. "I refuse to be ruffled by such insinuations," declared Jimmy. Claire looked in his direction sharply, amazed that he knew such big words. Then Jimmy thought he ought to be sensible at a time like this.

"What do you mean?" asked Claire quizzically, "You wanted to be early?" Jimmy looked at Claire and took a deep breath, rolling his eyes skyward, as if to say 'Oh no! Not you too!'

"Well!" he said in an attempt to try to explain himself, "David asked me to be here for seven o'clock.... and I arrived bang on seven. Now," he said, using his hands to express himself to the full. "If, as he professes I'm always late, then in my book, I must be early.... right?"

"Right!" confirmed Claire, with delight. She couldn't hide the pleasure she felt at Jimmy getting 'one over' on her brother, beating him at his own game.

David silently admitted defeat. "All right!" he said moodily as he gathered his thoughts. "I asked you round to discuss Bella.... and what we ought to be doing to help."

Jimmy took off his anorak and joined David sitting on the floor. "So!" Jimmy sighed disappointedly, "You've had no news of Bella then?" His friend sounded more friendly towards him now.

"No!" I telephoned the radio station this morning to see if there was any news.... but they've heard nothing."

"It's a complete mystery," said Claire, who sat cross legged and with her arms folded, and looked as if she was at a Red Indian pow-wow.

Jimmy was stumped. "A dog can't just disappear into thin air, can it?" he asked, not really expecting an answer.

"Bella has!" said David.

His sister looking worried asked, "What if she's never found? What do we do then?"

David placed his elbows on the table disturbing the pieces of Scrabble but no one even noticed, "I don't know," he said, "but we'll have to think of something. They then sat in gloomy silence.

After a while, Jimmy broke the silence, saying, "What about poor Tom? How is he going to get around without a guide dog?"

David shrugged his shoulders, "We'll just have to get him another one, that's all."

Marion Jeffries peeped over the top of the evening paper she was reading. "David?" she frowned, "Do you know how much they cost?"

"No!" replied her son, but I imagine they would cost about one hundred pounds."

His mother put her paper down. "I'm sorry to disappoint you dear, but they are more likely to cost around one thousand pounds."

The children gulped in disbelief. "A thousand pounds?" they asked in unison.

"How on earth are we going to raise that amount of money?" asked Claire, still reeling from shock.

But her brother was determined. "We'll just jolly well have to find a way - that's all" David's qualities of leadership were evident once again and he thought deeply for a moment. "What about all the hard work Tom did to raise money for other people who were blind.... so that they could have a guide dog to help them." He looked serious as he spoke. "I think the least we could do is to try to raise enough money to get him another guide dog." Claire and Jimmy agreed.

However, Mrs Jeffries wasn't too sure of the procedure for getting another guide dog. "Just a minute, dear," not wishing to stifle their enthusiasm, "I have a feeling there is a system within the Guide Dog Association whereby they allocate their guide dogs according to the situation, or the most in need, or even by numbers on the application list."

David looked a little deflated. "I know," he said, "but that could take ages.... and besides, someone has to pay for the guide dog."

Jimmy was quick to add, "And poor Tom will be at the bottom of the list."

Claire agreed. "I think the only way we can be sure of getting Tom another guide dog, is to raise the money as soon as possible. After all, he is used to having a guide dog." Claire drew circles on the polished coffee table with her index finger. "He once told me," she said, "that he would never use a white stick again.... not after having Bella."

David had made his decision. "Right! That settles it! We will raise the money.... somehow."

Claire sat with her hands on her chin and sighed. "But, where do we begin?"

David had a sudden sparkle in his voice, "Don't you remember what Tom taught us?" Jimmy and Claire looked a little baffled until David explained. "Where there's a will.... there's a way."

All were agreed they would put into practice all that Tom had taught them, including the three D's: Desire, Determination and Do.

"Come on then," said David, "let's get our heads together and think up some ideas for raising funds." He looked at his sister with a brotherly smile, "Claire, perhaps you could rustle up some pencils and paper, then we can make up a list of our plans."

Claire willingly did as her brother asked and within minutes they were each sat in front of a blank piece of paper, each struggling for inspiration.

"Come on, brain, think!" said a stumped Jimmy running his pencil through his short haircut.

Marion Jeffries had almost finished reading her evening paper, and she put it down to help the children with their ideas. "If it's of any help to you," she offered, "I have an idea." The children looked up, anxiously waiting. "If we need to raise funds at the WI Club, we hold a Bring and Buy sale. I know it is not very original but we always seem to make lots of money."

"Hey! Yes!" said David eagerly, "that's a good idea." They all wrote it down on their lists.

"What about a Summer Fayre?" asked Claire excitedly.

Jimmy couldn't resist quipping, "What? In autumn? Be a bit cold for the white elephant."

Claire was not amused. "All right!" she retorted, "An Autumn Fayre, then."

David agreed an Autumn Fayre was a good idea. He suggested they ask Mr Mason if they could use the school hall. Then they began to list the various types of stalls and the games that would be needed.

Claire suddenly had a burst of enthusiasm and almost shouted, "I know, I could sell balloons.... on second thoughts," she sighed, "I'm not very good at art.... but I could paint spots on them and call them polkadot balloons."

Jimmy put his hands on his hips and sighed, "Spotty balloons?" he joked, "You won't sell many - people will think they've got measles." David and his mother laughed but Claire did not care to see the funny side of Jimmy's joke and she shot him a look of contempt as her enthusiasm waned.

"Of course," said David thoughtfully, "you could make it a bit more exciting by painting numbers on the balloons and having a prize for the lucky number at the end of the day." Claire smiled once more.

David fidgeted with his pencil, "But then," he said, "we're going to need lots of help to run these stalls."

Claire's brain was working overtime now, "How about a wishing well?" she asked excitedly.

"That would make one hundred per cent profit." Marion

Jeffries was the first to see the potential of Claire's idea. "Well done! Claire," she praised her young daughter for giving profit top priority. David agreed, but wondered who they could get to run the wishing well. Claire seized the opportunity.

"How about Jimmy?" she giggled, but Jimmy wasn't laughing.

"You must be joking!" he retorted in a high pitched voice. "You can get one of the girls to do that." There was definite pleasure in his voice as he turned to David. "How about Rosie.... eh, David?" But David didn't bite Jimmy's bait. He remained calm and in control.

"All right!" David agreed, surprising his friend, "That's Rosie on the wishing well." They all wrote notes accordingly. "Now," said David, "what about Jimmy? We have to think of something for you."

"I know!" cried Claire, "Indoor skittles!" She laughed as she explained, "We could stand him up and they could knock him down." Marion Jeffries smiled as she picked up the evening paper again to read once more.

"Oh! Very funny Claire," said Jimmy huffily. He didn't mind handing the jokes out but didn't like being the butt of other people's jokes.... especially Claire's. "Any more wisecracks like that," he threatened, "and I'll pop all of your balloons."

David was quick to diffuse the situation. "Come on," he said, "we haven't got time to fool around." The three of them sat in silence as they tried to think of more stalls and games.

Marion Jeffries interrupted the silence. "If it's of any help, dear," she said looking at David, "I could make some cakes... come to think of it, I could ask the ladies at the WI to help out. I'm sure they wouldn't mind once they know what it is for."

"That would be a great help. Thanks! Mum," replied David gratefully.

"We could hold a raffle, too," enthused Claire, "they

always make a lot of money." They all agreed with Claire's idea.

Jimmy was spurred into action now, "What about Guess the sweets?" he asked. "We can fill a jar with Dolly Mixtures and people can guess how many sweets there are in the jar. We could charge five pence a guess... and make a good profit." Once again the others agreed and they all wrote it in their notes.

"I could ask some friends to help me make Christmas cards and gift tags out of last year's Christmas cards and they wouldn't cost anything to make," said Claire.

"Good thinking! Claire," said her brother, before offering an idea of his own. "I've just had an idea!" said David in a serious tone. He always commanded Jimmy and Claire's respect when he was serious. "We could go to all the shops and stores locally to ask them if they would be kind enough to donate at least one item from their stock, and then..." He was now becoming excited by the idea. "Then we could auction them off at the fayre." This idea certainly caused the most excitement. "Can I be the auctioneer?" asked Jimmy, waving his pencil in the air.

"All right!" agreed David. Claire was at a loss for words; at times like this she had to admit David was clever.

"David," she said with a wry smile, "I think when brains were handed out you must have jumped the queue."

Jimmy pipped in, "Yes, and us lesser mortals have to make do with second best."

David felt a glow inside as his mother complimented him on a brilliant idea.... one that could well be the star attraction at the fayre. David decided it should be called the 'Name Your Price' auction. All agreed. David frowned, "You know we should hold this Fayre soon."

Jimmy added, "The sooner the better."

Claire asked, "What about this Saturday?"

Her brother pursed his lips before saying, "Oooh! That might be pushing it a bit. Although," he said as though he had had second thoughts, "we should be able to get lots of help, so it might be possible."

Claire almost knocked the coffee table over as she jumped up excitedly. "I've got a brilliant idea!" she cried and as her face lit up, her eyes grew into two big pools of happiness. "How about us putting on a School Disco? That would be all profit."

Her brother looked amazed. He hadn't realised his sister was capable of such intelligence. "Brilliant! Claire." he said in a proud voice.

Jimmy grinned, "You're not just a pretty face Claire.... are you?" Claire accepted Jimmy's compliments with a pinch of salt.... she knew they were easier to digest that way.

Marion Jeffries folded the newspaper and put it down beside her. "Well!" she said as she stretched in her chair, "From the sound of things you are all going to be extremely busy between now and Saturday."

David had a determined look on his face.... a look his mother knew so well. "Yes," he said cautiously, "but it can be done.... if everyone puts their minds to it."

Jimmy sighed, "Well, today's Monday, so we barely have a week."

"But.... we have lots of friends to help," said an optimistic Claire.

As Mrs Jeffries went out into the kitchen to make them a hot drink, they all agreed on one thing, Tom would need another guide dog... and soon, if Bella wasn't found, and there was no time to waste.

"Where there's a will!" said David, and the three of them echoed, "There's a way!"

99

CHAPTER EIGHT: FOR A VERY WORTHY CAUSE

Every day the children had enquired after Bella but there was no sign of her. Tom was beside himself with grief and, although numerous friends and acquaintances called to offer practical help, he was inconsolable. The children from Seaton High School realised that they had to carry out their plans as soon as possible.

Saturday morning arrived with a welcome package of blue skies and sunshine, and although there had been a heavy ground frost overnight, the sun shone to warm the hearts of all the kind people involved in organising the Autumn Fayre. Mr Mason, along with a couple of young helpers, was erecting the AUTUMN FAYRE sign outside the main entrance to the school. They had hung red, white and blue flags around the hall which was a hive of activity. It looked very much like a fairground with all the colourful stalls and sideshows. David, with all his many helpers and friends had put a tremendous amount of work into getting the Fayre ready on time. They had decided to hold the School Disco on the following Tuesday evening.

Mr Mason had been kind enough to print and photocopy hundreds of hand bills with the relevant details. These had been sent to all parents of children in the school, ensuring they were aware of the two fund-raising events, and hopefully would support them.

David, Claire, Melanie, Jimmy, along with Basher and Little Tim, were all putting the finishing touches to their respective stalls and side-shows before going home for some well-earned lunch. They had two hours before the Fayre opened at two o'clock.

At half-past-one the sun was still shining. Melanie was returning to school when she met Rosie coming along the road, struggling with a load of parcels. Well, she thought it looked like Rosie, but she could hardly see her friend's face; all she could see was the top of her head, blue jeans and white trainers. Rosie caught sight of Melanie out of one eye... through a gap in the parcels, and suddenly plonked the lot down on the pavement with a "Phew!"

"Hello Rosie!" called Melanie. "What on earth have you got there?"

"Hi Melanie!" said Rosie, still puffing and panting trying to get her breath back. "These are all for the Auction this afternoon."

"Oh!" said Melanie, as Rosie arched her aching back, "David and Jimmy wouldn't go into the ladies' shops.... so they sent muggins here."

"Typical of boys!" Melanie said as she peered over to see what Rosie had managed to get for the Auction. "Did you manage to get anything nice?"

"Yes!" said Rosie sounding quite pleased with herself. "I've got... a ladies' electric shaver, some heated hair rollers; some soap and talc sets and some perfume; a frilly nightie and a travelling hair dryer...." she said pointing to the relevant packages.

"Where is it travelling to?" she asked, trying to keep a straight face.

It took Rosie a moment to realise what her friend had said. "Oh Melanie" she laughed and then continued. "Now, what else have I got? Oh yes, there's a matching handbag and purse; a make-up bag, some dusting powder, a manicure set; and, oh yes," she concluded, "a lovely vanity case."

Melanie's eyes grew bigger with the list. "Golly!" she gasped, "You have done well. I've been up at school since nine o'clock this morning making a stand for all the Christmas cards and gift tags." She leaned closer to Rosie as if to confide in her. "I managed to persuade the whole of the art class to paint cards for me." She giggled, then shrugged her delicately formed shoulders. "Well!" she said defensively, "I would never have had them all done on time... David didn't give us long, did he?.... A week! that's all."

Rosie agreed with her friend, and yet, she wanted to defend David's motives. "I know it has all been a bit of a rush," she said, tossing her woollen scarf around her neck, "but I can see David's point.... If Bella isn't found soon Tom is going to need another guide dog to replace her."

Melanie looked sad. "But he could never replace Bella," she said with a frown clouding her pretty face. Rosie smiled, reassuring her friend that although Tom could never replace Bella, he would need another guide dog to help him get around, and he would need one soon. Melanie stared at the pavement for a moment. "What I can't understand," she said, "is why no one has seen her." She turned to gaze at Rosie. "It has been in all the papers, so everyone must know that Bella is still missing."

Rosie felt her eyes mist as she spoke in a gentle voice. "Poor Bella," she said softly, as the happy memory of a playful Bella in the park flashed through her mind, "and poor Tom too," she said, "He's taken it badly. Of course, someone must have enticed her into their home and is keeping her hidden."

Melanie frowned, "But why would anyone want to do that?"

"Well," said Rosie, trying to be practical, "Bella is a famous guide dog and someone could be jealous of her." She shrugged her shoulders, "Who knows what some people will do? Or why?"

"I just hope they have a conscience," said Melanie, sounding much older than her eleven years. Rosie agreed, then looked at her watch and realised that the time was getting on and she still had lots to do. "I hope the Fayre's a huge success," said Rosie. "So do I," added Melanie. She offered to help Rosie with the parcels and they struggled on towards the school together.

It was almost two o'clock as the helpers were putting the finishing touches to their stalls. Mr Mason checked his watch. At precisely two o'clock he asked if everyone was ready, before opening the doors to the main entrance of the hall. A crowd of people, some of whom had been queuing up since one o'clock, surged through the open door with an air of bustling excitement. They had all heard about the star prize, plus the other goodies they could win.

The sound of the stall holders' cries suddenly filled the hall. Basher and Little Tim, who were in charge of Topple The Topper were crying in full voice.... "Topple the Topper.... Topple the Topper.... Double your money if you Topple the Topper." Basher stood inside a ringed area with a huge black top hat on his head, while Little Tim stood outside the ropes with a seaside bucket full of tennis balls and a large notice that said '5p A THROW'. Melanie was in good voice also, "Christmas cards, gift tags, wrapping paper. Come now... buy for Christmas." She repeated this between serving each customer. She had been very busy making the stand as attractive as possible; knowing that that was the secret of getting the crowds around her stall and selling well. The hand-painted cards were selling very well at 50p each and she was sure that they would boost her total cash at the end of the day.

Jimmy could be seen and heard walking around with the raffle tickets and his cash tin, shouting, "Raffle Tickets! Raffle Tickets! Ten pence each or a pound for ten.... for the Mystery Prize. Roll up! Roll up! Get your raffle tickets now if you would like to win the Star Prize." He was suddenly silenced by a host of hands all wanting to try their luck.

David was busy checking that everything was ready for the Auction which was to be held in the second part of the afternoon. While he had a few minutes to spare he decided to go to each person on their allotted stalls to see how they were faring. His mother had delegated some of the work on the cake stall to other members of the WI, while she helped out spinning the wheel on the Wheel of Fortune. The spinning wheel was very colourful in red and gold, with pockets attached to the outer edge of the wheel; the wheel spun in one direction while the large arrow in the centre of the wheel spun in the opposite direction. When the two stopped spinning, the number the arrow came to rest upon was the number of the pocket which held the envelope containing the prize. Marion Jeffries would then read out the 'fortune' to whoever was the winner. It was amazing how many people were interested to know what Lady Luck had in store for them. Claire looked as if she was drowning in a sea of balloons. However, her lilting voice still carried, "Lucky Balloons! Lucky Balloons.... Who will buy my Lucky Balloons?" She repeated her call over and over again, between sales. She held a bunch of polka-dot balloons in each hand while four bunches floated in the air, held fast to the sturdy stand that Mr Mason had made for her. Each balloon had a number hidden in among the polka-dots. Claire was careful to tell all her customers not to lose their balloon, as towards the end of the Fayre there would be a draw to find the winning number.

Rosie joined in the harmony of stall cries with, "Wishing Well! Wishing Well! Come make a wish in the Wishing Well." She stood beside a large red and green brick wishing well, complete with ratchet handle and suspended bucket. Alas, not many people were throwing money into the wishing well. She tried hard to think of an alternative method of attracting customers. Apart from standing on her pretty head, she couldn't think of anything. Then she had a bright idea. She remembered seeing buskers in the town on Saturdays and people throwing money into their violin case. She desperately wanted to please David and help raise plenty of money and if that meant singing to bring people over to the wishing well, then that's what she would do.

After giving it careful consideration she decided on a song that she felt would be appropriate, entitled 'Try A Little Wishing'. She knew she would have to choose her timing and waited for a lull in the stall cries so that she would be heard throughout the hall. Suddenly Rosie burst into song to the amazement of everyone in the hall. The melody carried through the hall. Rosie was a talented little singer and she felt confident as she sang her heart out.

"Would you like to throw a penny in the wishing well
You can toss in any coin and make a wish as well
If you have a dream you're dreaming - one you
cannot tell
Try a little wishing then, in my secret wishing well
If your dream is in your heart, then make a wish or two
Maybe someone else will wish to make your dreams
come true
Wishing wells are made for wishing - anyone can tell
All you have to do is wish.... in the Wishing Well."

Rosie was soon surrounded by a small group of people,
which was getting larger by the minute. Suddenly everyone
wanted to know what was going on over by the Wishing
Well: Rosie was thrilled, she had a captive audience. As she
burst into the final chorus of her song, some of the people
surrounding her joined in. David stood quietly in the
background with a feeling he couldn't explain, as he listened
to Rosie sing.

"If your dream is in your heart, then make a wish or two
Maybe someone else will wish to make your dreams
come true
Wishing wells are made for wishing - anyone can tell
All you have to do is wish.... in the Wishing Well."

The applause that followed was deafening. They loved
Rosie. Suddenly everyone wanted to throw money in the
wishing well. One five year old boy, having thrown his
money in and closed his eyes to wish, then came running up
to Rosie and told her he had wished she would be his
girlfriend. Rosie positively glowed as she smiled, continuing
to change notes into coins for eager customers. Her mother
and father were in the background too, listening to their
daughter of whom they were very proud. They moved on,
not wishing to embarrass Rosie with their compliments in
front of strangers.

Rosie's Mum decided she would have her fortune told. They both went over to the Wheel of Fortune where Mrs Jeffries was still spinning the wheel. Marion knew Mr and Mrs Painter, of course, and was full of compliments for their talented young daughter. The arrow stopped at number seven and she took the envelope from the pocket on the outer wheel and read it out. "You should take full advantage of all opportunities that come your way, because... today could be your lucky day."

"There you are!" said Mrs Painter to her husband, "I told you I felt lucky today." She winked at Marion, "I think I'll have a go on everything here today."

"I should if I were you," laughed Marion Jeffries before turning to attend to her next customer.

The school hall was a hive of activity as the Fayre got into full swing. Mr Mason was being kept busy on the Indoor Skittles, which seemed to be a hit with the younger children. In fact, all the stalls and games were in great demand.

David managed to make his way through the jostling people towards Claire, who was looking flushed and delighted. "How are you doing, Claire?"

"Great!" called Claire. "They're selling like hot cakes." She shook her money tin that was getting heavy and watched her brother smile.

"Well done!" he said. He had a quiet confidence that the Fayre was going to be a success. He looked across the hall with eyes that were searching for someone. "Where's that Jimmy Lucas?" he asked no one in particular. He then called across to Claire and asked if she had seen Jimmy. Claire replied that she had been much too busy to worry about Jimmy Lucas. Eventually David spotted Jimmy talking - as only he could - to a group of girls. David went across and shouted, "Come on, Jimmy, we have to get the Auction started." Jimmy quickly made his excuses to his fan club and joined David.

"Everybody wants me," he said, shrugging his

shoulders, "It must be my charm."

There were times when David found himself agreeing with his sister that Jimmy Lucas could be a pain at times. "Come on," said David impatiently, "we have to get the show rolling."

"What shall I do with these?" asked Jimmy as he suddenly realised that he still had the raffle tickets and money tin with him.

"Ask Mr Mason if he will look after them for you."

Jimmy was back in no time and becoming excited about being the auctioneer. He had spent the best part of the day before looking in a mirror, practising and now he felt fairly confident. David checked that everything was ready before ringing the heavy school bell he had borrowed.

"Ladies and gentlemen!" he shouted. No one could fail to hear the large brass bell. "It is now time for our Auction." As the hall suddenly went quieter, he felt he had the attention of the majority of people. "If you would all like to gather round, we can start the auction." He paused until a group had gathered around the stall. "We have some very exciting items for you in our auction." He pointed to them as he listed them one by one. "We have a colour television set; a radio cassette recorder; a sandwich toaster; a car vacuum cleaner; vanity case and gift sets; a lovely painting.... and lots more." David went on to explain that all the items had been very generously donated by local shops to help raise funds to provide another guide dog for Mr Sinclair. "So come on," he shouted, "if you will gather round we will start the bidding." He looked at Jimmy who was poised and ready for action. "Over to you Jimmy."

David was stunned as he witnessed his friend as an auctioneer. Jimmy began with the television set. "Who will start the bidding at one pound? Thank you, madam! One pound! Two... Three.... Four pounds! Five! Six! Seven pounds! Eight! Nine! Ten pounds!" The adrenalin was beginning to flow and Jimmy was enjoying himself as hands started to wave anxiously in front of him. "Ten pounds I am offered any advance on ten pounds? Ten pounds... Fifteen! Eighteen! Twenty pounds! Twenty-five! That's more like it!" he shouted, "Now you're alive! Thirty! Forty! Forty-five pounds! Fifty, do I hear fifty? Fifty pounds! Thank you, sir! Any advance on fifty? Come on make me one more bid." Jimmy scanned the crowd to see if there were any more bids, but he saw none. "Now its going for a song.... Going.... Going.... GONE!" He brought his hand-made hammer down with a thump to indicate that that was the conclusion of the bidding for the television set. "Sold to the man in the navy blue blazer. Thank you, Sir." David was in charge of the cash and goods side of the auction and looked every bit the part in his woodworking apron with its large 'kangaroo pouch' pocket. He dealt with the sale of the television set while Jimmy went into his auctioneer routine once again.

Claire and Rosie who were still manning their own stalls, looked at each other in amazement. They could not believe that Jimmy Lucas could be sensible long enough to be such a competent auctioneer. The auction turned out to be the highlight of the afternoon and a great success, raising a considerable amount of money. David and Jimmy managed to sell every item.

Finally, David rang the large brass bell once more for attention. "Thank you, ladies and gentlemen!" When he was sure he had their attention he continued... "I would just like to thank you all for coming here this afternoon and making our Autumn Fayre such a success." He smiled, "I hope that you have all had fun and found a bargain or two. I can assure you that every penny raised here today will go towards the cost of a new guide dog for Mr Tom Sinclair." He paused for breath, "However, should Bella be found in the meantime.... and we pray she will be.... then the money will go to the Guide Dogs for the Blind Association - a very worthy cause." There was a resounding "Here! Here!" from the crowd.

As they applauded, David suddenly remembered.... "Now, before you leave, there is just one other thing.... and

I'm sure it's the moment for which you have all been waiting." He smiled at the crowd and then shouted out.... 'The draw for the Mystery Prize!" David then called across to Mr Mason asking if he would be kind enough to draw for the Star Prize. Jimmy, in the meantime, retrieved the revolving drum from under the auction stand in preparation and Mrs Jeffries quickly placed all the folded raffle tickets inside.... ready for the lucky spin, as Mr Mason made his way through the crowd to the table. "First of all, Sir," said David, holding out a large white envelope, "perhaps you would like to reveal what is the Mystery Prize."

"Why, yes, of course," said a smiling Mr Mason, "I'd be delighted," and he proceeded to open the envelope. "The Mystery Prize is.... A Fabulous Holiday for two in the sunny Isle of Minorca!" There were gasps of "Ooohs!" and "Aaahs!" from the crowd as Mr Mason continued.... 'The prize consists of two whole weeks in one of Minorca's luxury hotels.... All expenses paid. Just think," he said, wishing he had found time to buy some tickets himself, "two whole weeks of glorious sunshine.... just what I could do with!"

He turned to David who was now giving the drum a jolly good spin, "Now! Let's see who is the lucky winner." Once the drum had stopped spinning, he closed his eyes and reached inside for a single ticket. "And the winning number is.... a pink ticket, number Sixty eight!" There was a moment's silence as everyone checked their tickets until Mr Mason saw a hand being waved at the back of the hall.

"It's me!" cried a jubilant Mrs Painter. As she approached, she turned around and called out to her husband, "I told you it was my lucky day."

Rosie called across the hall, "Well done, Mum!"

As Mrs Painter reached the stand Mr Mason congratulated her and gave her all the details of the flight and hotel. "Ooh!" she said, visibly flushed. "How marvellous! Thank you very much." There were cheers and hand clapping as she made her way back to her husband's side.

As the applause subsided Mr Mason addressed the crowd once more. "Well, I'm afraid that's all for now, ladies and gentlemen. However, I would like to say thank you all for coming. As David has already told you, all the money raised here today will go towards another guide dog for Mr Sinclair. We pray that Bella returns, of course, and in which case the money will go to the Guide Dogs for the Blind Association.

I would just like to make a small point here, and that is that the Guide Dog Association relies entirely on donations from the public and do a marvellous job breeding, training and maintaining the high standard of their dogs. More and more blind people are able to lead normal lives through being able to 'see' once more through the eyes of their guide dogs. Although each dog costs around one thousand pounds to train, the Association continue to maintain the dogs once they are placed with their new owners, paying for food and vets' fees. This, of course, alleviates the financial worry for the owner of a guide dog." He smiled, and went on, "The Association do make a charge.... of fifty pence which the blind person pays. However, this is merely a token charge. So you see, the Guide Dogs for the Blind Association do a fantastic job but they do need much public support to carry on their work." He paused for breath and then continued... "We're all aware of the bond that can be forged between a blind person and their dog, as we have seen with Tom and Bella." There were nods of agreement.

Mr Mason concluded, "And so I take this opportunity to thank each and every one of you for your support. I do hope you have enjoyed yourselves. Incidentally, I think we should give a big hand to all the children who have worked so hard to put this Fayre on today, especially our auctioneers." He looked across at an embarrassed David and Jimmy. "I thought they were terrific," he said admiringly, "didn't you?"

David looked in every direction as he avoided the eyes of so many admiring girls. Suddenly, his wavering gaze caught Rosie' s smiling eyes. Then he looked momentarily at his friend Jimmy with a grin of satisfaction and slapped him on the back, knowing all their hard work had paid off. David's eyes scanned the cheering crowd before finding Rosie' s smile once more. She was so proud of him. There, in the middle of an extended applause, they were alone - in a magic world of their own.

CHAPTER NINE: RAISING THE ROOF

The school bus pulled up outside Seaton High School gates and out poured the first batch of schoolchildren to arrive. It was Monday morning, the weather was dank and miserable but the children' s spirits were high. They chatted excitedly about the events of Saturday's Autumn Fayre wondering how much money they had raised.

Marion Jeffries walked as far as the school with David and Claire on her way to the bank in Seaton' s High Street to deposit the money raised at the Fayre. Sensibly, she had put the money in the night safe of the bank on her way home on Saturday after the Fayre; it was too much to have lying around the house over the weekend. Just past the school gates Mrs Jeffries recognised Mr Mason coming towards her.

"Hello! Mrs Jeffries. I was hoping I might see you this morning. What was the final figure on Saturday?" The games teacher shivered in the cold air.

"Good morning, Mr Mason! I'm just on my way to the bank. You'll be delighted to know.... the grand total is seven hundred and twenty pounds and eighty-two pence. Don't you think that is tremendous?" A radiant Marion positively glowed with delight.

"I certainly do. That's marvellous! And I have to say what a grand job David, Claire and their friends have done." He shook his head in admiration. "It's incredible the way they have rallied round to help Tom. It really does my heart good to see such spirit still exists in the youth of today."

Marion smiled proudly. 'Thank you, Mr Mason! I must admit I was proud of them too. And, of course, there is still the school disco to come, that should raise a few more pounds."

"I'm sure it will." Mr Mason rubbed his beard in thought. "I've asked David to be finished by half-past-ten. Can't have them missing lessons the next day, can we?" he teased.

Marion smiled, "No! Not even if it is for a good cause." They both laughed. "Funny business, if you ask me," he said as the smile drained from his handsome face, "I think someone has taken Bella in and now they don't want to let her go and, of course, as time goes on they will be too afraid to because of the repercussions from public opinion and media attention."

"Poor Bella!" said Marion thoughtfully. "If they thought for a moment how inseparable Tom and Bella were, they might have second thoughts about keeping her."

"Oh well!" concluded the PE teacher, "I suppose there is still time." He looked at his watch, "I must be going, but I'll let you know if I hear anything. It's been nice talking to you. 'Bye for now!"

Marion Jeffries smiled as she said goodbye to a man for whom she had a certain admiration. Her shiny blonde hair bobbed as she walked briskly towards the bank in the High Street. However, there was a nagging thought which dominated her mood now; Bella had been missing for ten days.... and yet she had not been sighted anywhere. Marion felt that there was something uncanny about Bella's total disappearance. The police had received no reports of a dog being involved in an accident on any of the roads in the area and with all the publicity not one person had come forward to say they had seen her.

On the spur of the moment, as she left the bank, Marion decided to visit Tom. She felt sure he would be glad of some company. However, she decided not to tell him about the Autumn Fayre nor about the School Disco. She thought he might see it as negative action, when he was trying hard to be positive: there was no way he would give up on Bella after only ten days.

It was raining miserably by the time a subdued Tom opened the front door to Marion. He was quietly pleased to think David's mother had taken the time to visit him. As he invited her into the living room she could not help thinking that she had never seen such a change in a man. Tom had gone from a happy, carefree, confident and lively person to a sad and lonely, desolate figure. Tom without Bella, was like a bird with a broken wing.

Tom switched the electric fire on for Marion, he seemed to think it was a waste of time putting it on just for himself. He accepted Marion's offer to make them both a cup of hot coffee.Then they sat by the fire talking about the children.... about the weather.... anything but Bella.

Tom sipped his warming coffee and felt suddenly comforted by the warmth of the fire and a kind, sympathetic ear. Marion then asked how he was bearing up in the circumstances. He, of course, said he was fine. However, Marion could obviously see that he was not.

"By the way," said Tom, pointing in the direction of the telephone table, "there's a letter by the telephone, I wonder if you would be kind enough to read it to me?"

"Yes, of course," said Marion pleased to be able to help. She picked up the letter and returned to her seat by the fire, opposite Tom, and began to read:

"It's from a Mrs Boardman in Chesterton." She could see that Tom recognised the writer.

"Good Lord!" he said, his tired eyes opening wide. 'That's Bella's puppy-walker!" and he tilted his head towards Marion to be sure to hear every word as she continued:

"Dear Mr Sinclair,

I can't begin to tell you how sorry I was to learn of Bella's disappearance. I can imagine how you must be suffering. I too have wept since hearing the news. I wanted so much to ring you when I first heard the news, but I would have been of little comfort to you the way I felt. You see, I too loved Bella."

Marion paused for a moment and looked up to see tears

rolling down Tom's cheeks. She hesitated. "Do you want me to carry on, Tom?"

"Yes, please," he said, brushing his tears aside. Marion cleared her throat and continued:

> "As Bella's puppy-walker I had the privilege of rearing her for the nine months allotted time for puppy walking and, in that short time, I grew more attached to Bella than to any of my previous or, indeed, subsequent charges. I knew then that she was a very special dog. When she left me I had a very heavy heart. At the same time though she left me richer.... richer for having known and loved her. She was one in a million.
>
> I am in touch with the local Guide Dog training centre,who are kindly keeping me informed and I pray with all my heart that Bella will turn up soon. If there is anything I can do, anything at all, please don't hesitate to let me know.
>
> All my heartfelt best wishes to you,
> From,
> Phyllis Boardman."

Marion swallowed a lump in her throat as she folded the letter neatly and placed it back in its envelope. 'That was a very moving letter," she sighed.

Tom sniffed in an attempt to suppress his tears. "Yes, it was, wasn't it?" He placed his handkerchief back in his pocket, then sat in silence, digesting the contents of the letter. Marion was acutely aware of the silence; she knew that she would have to draw Tom's feelings out if she was going to be of any real help.

"You haven't given up, Tom, have you?" There was a tenderness in Marion's voice to which Tom responded.

"No" he said quietly. Then, as if mustering his last bit of strength he sat up straight in his chair and sighed. "It's just that I am afraid," he said, looking in the direction of Bella's

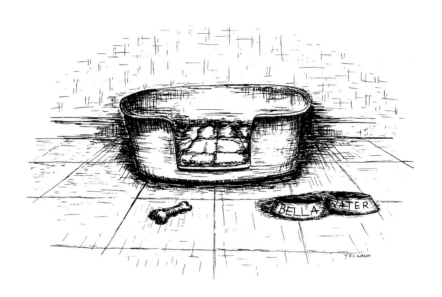

empty bed. He swallowed hard. "It's now ten days since Bella went missing, and no one seems to have seen her anywhere." He wrung his hands, "Even the appeal didn't work, did it?"

Marion felt like putting her arms around the blind man to protect him from the pain she knew he was going through. "Listen, Tom," she said softly, in the hope that she could lift his spirits a little, "have you thought about seeing a clairvoyant?" She wasn't even sure if Tom was against such things.

"No," he said, with a vague expression on his now lined, pale, face.

"Well, they have been known to find missing people, and so it's possible, just possible, that they could find a missing dog."

Tom seemed to perk up for a moment. "I wonder?" he said, rubbing his unshaven chin as he digested the idea.

Marion was quick to add that she knew of one in the High Street, who was reputed to be very good. Tom eagerly agreed to give it a try. Marion thumbed through Tom's telephone directory for Madame Francesca's number and before Tom could change his mind she rang and made an appointment for two o'clock on Wednesday afternoon. Marion assured Tom that she would take him but that David and Claire would meet him afterwards, as she had a pre arranged hair appointment. Marion was pleased to see a little colour return to Tom's cheeks.

"Do you really think she might be able to help?", Tom asked. "It would be wonderful if this Madame Francesca could find Bella for me." He looked skyward for a moment, and said, "then all my prayers would be answered."

Marion witnessed a definite lift in Tom's spirits and felt a glow of satisfaction that she had been able to give this lovely man a little hope. "I must be off now, Tom," she smiled, as she put on her coat. "I'll pick you up at half past one on Wednesday. She bent over and caught hold of Tom's hand and squeezed it gently as she said in a low voice, "I'll say a little prayer for you."

"Bless you!" Tom said, "for giving me a little hope."

Marion Jeffries walked the mile or so back home with a bounce in her step and a smile in her heart knowing she had cheered up Tom a little.

* * * * *

Tuesday evening arrived all too soon for some of the mothers who were frantically putting the finishing touches to fancy dress costumes. Claire had suggested that those attending the school disco should appear in fancy dress as this would add more fun to the evening. They planned to hold a competition for the most original costume, hence the pressure on mothers to work minor miracles in a matter of days.

David managed to get in touch with a famous local pop group, called The Rocking Mind Blowers. The group had an engagement booked, but once David told them about the cause they agreed to do a ten minute spot at the disco before going on to their booking in town. They said they would have to use a backing tape as there would be no time for setting up all their equipment. However, David was only too happy to accept this, being delighted that they were able to put in an appearance at all.

It was seven-fifteen when the first group of children arrived in fancy dress. David looked dashing in a soldier's combat jacket and trousers complete with camouflage helmet and webbing. Claire arrived as Lady Godiva, dressed in a flesh-coloured body stocking, with her long blonde hair flowing loosely about her shoulders. Jimmy Lucas breezed in dressed as a comical version of the famous artist, Van Gogh. It was a simple but very original idea. His outsize smock was daubed with various coloured paints. He sported a moustache and wore a beret that was much too large for him and kept falling over his ears; he also carried a palette and brush. David thought he was hilarious and it certainly made a good start to the evening.

As more and more children began to arrive, the hall was filling with screams of laughter, proving that Claire's idea

118

was paying off. They were having more fun in the first ten minutes of the disco than they had had for months. Claire busied herself with setting up the refreshments' stall and she was in her element. The budding caterer had arranged for half-a-dozen friends to bake cakes and helped to make sandwiches to donate to the disco, again helping to boost funds for the night. There was also a crate of lemonade that had been donated by a local supermarket, together with paper cups.

Basher was at the door in charge of entrance fees, dressed aptly as Al Capone. He wore a black shirt with a flashy tie. There was the obvious trilby hat tilted at an angle over his eyes and an oversize jacket into which his mother had sewn shoulder pads. He had painted a black moustache for authenticity; he certainly looked the part as he made sure everyone paid their pound entrance fee. No one tried to slip through without paying as they knew the name Basher would mean 'Bouncer'.

David with help from Little Tim was setting up the disco lights around a table they had borrowed from the dining hall. He had brought along a record player and a selection of hit records gathered from various friends. Mr Mason had been in to check on the safety of all the electrical equipment during the afternoon, and to make sure that there were no trailing wires likely to cause accidents. David tested the school microphone which he had managed to borrow - he knew he would be needing it with fifty children to organise, their ages ranging from ten to fourteen. They were all excited, more so because of the fancy dress and trying to find out just who was in the more outrageous costumes.

"All right, Tim," said David, "let's start the music." Suddenly the music blared out through two large speakers and in no time at all everyone was dancing. Being in fancy dress helped many shed their inhibitions and they were all doing their own thing on the dance floor.

Rosie looked a romantic figure in a uniform of the Women's Royal Army Corps, complete with pips on her shoulders: nothing less than officer status for Rosie. She plucked up courage to grab a busy David from the disco rostrum and ask him to dance. He was bashful but happily agreed. He felt a flush in his cheeks, this was like something he'd read in magazines. He was falling in love, and he knew it.

As the record ended David rushed back to the rostrum and took hold of the microphone. "Are you all enjoying yourselves?" he shouted. The response almost drowned the introduction of the next record. "Good!" shouted David. They continued dancing for a further fifteen minutes, then David took the stand again.

"Now for the fancy dress competition," he said rubbing his hands together, "but don't worry he assured them all, we have lots more entertainment for you." David looked hard into the sea of storybook characters before spotting Jimmy Lucas, alias Van Gogh. The boys all had a field day with this news; their whistles drowned out David's voice. "Jimmy will walk among you and eliminate you.... one at a time." He took a breath before continuing, hoping the cheers would subdue. "Until there is only one person left and who, of course, will be the winner tonight. I know it won't be easy to judge the best of such a brilliant fancy dress turnout.... However, Jimmy will do his best."

David almost forgot "Incidentally" he concluded, "the prize for the competition winner will be tickets for two to see the film of your choice at the Empire Cinema." A cheer went up at this news.

David left the excited chatter to join Little Tim in a bid to chose the next record.

They chose a slow tune in order to give Jimmy time to study all the costumes. David started the music and Jimmy moved slowly among the dancers eliminating them one at a time. Finally, the music stopped and they had a winner.

"Hi! everybody," said Jimmy holding onto his falling

moustache, "As you can see we have our winner....and it is Spiderman!" Everyone cheered for Spiderman who was, indeed, a very worthy winner; Jimmy has chosen him because of his clever outfit. His mother and older brother had woven a spider's web in tinsel wool and pipe cleaners, which was attached to his back. All Jimmy could see of Spiderman was his eyes through the slits in his mask, which was black, as was the rest of his costume, with scaly markings all round.

"Congratulations! Spiderman!" shouted Jimmy, "You have won two tickets for the Empire Cinema.... to see a film of your choice." A delighted Spiderman accepted the envelope he was given, and waved it high in the air as he returned to his seat. Some of the children, including Spiderman, began taking off parts of their costumes; the dancing had made them hot and their costumes were becoming uncomfortable. As the clapping of hands subsided, Claire hurried across to David on the rostrum and whispered in his ear.

David immediately tested the microphone, "Can I please have your attention?" he asked.

Everyone looked towards him as he said, "We have a great surprise for you tonight." He smiled from ear to ear. "Will you please welcome our very special guests.... The Rocking Mind Blowers." He pointed in the direction of the double doors where the singing duo appeared. There were gasps of delight from the children who cheered their own real life rock stars, looking sensational in their trendy outfits.

This certainly was a surprise and the children sat enthralled. The duo entertained them for a good ten minutes, while some of the more impressionable girls gasped with delight. This was the highlight of the night, and as quickly as the duo had arrived - they were gone amid a hail of cheers and screams.

David took the microphone stand once more. "Weren't they great?" He fanned the air with his hands to quell the cheering and clapping. "You can all dance now. However, we do have some more entertainment for you a little later."

No one appeared to have noticed the absence of Basher and Melanie, who had slipped out to change ready for their 'spot' of entertaining.

Later, David called a halt to the dancing and asked for their full attention, saying, "Can you please give a big hand to The Copycats who will be dancing to The Valley of the Silhouettes."

There was a round of applause and a cheer as Melanie entered wearing her ballet attire and dancing beautifully as she took to the centre of the floor. Melanie had been attending ballet school since she was five years old and was, indeed, a very talented dancer. There was silence as everyone watched the dainty ballerina pirouetting.

Suddenly, the figure of Basher came bursting through the doors at the end of the hall. He was dressed in a mock ballet dress, two sizes too small for him and a wig of long blonde hair that fell loosely about his face. There was stunned silence before laughter erupted at the sight of him trying to mimic Melanie in his wellington boots, which looked as though they belonged to his father, and it was the funniest thing they had seen in a long time. Basher tried to follow every dainty step but failed: it was like something out of a cartoon. As Melanie executed her final pirouette, Basher tried hopelessly to follow in her shadow, but in doing so he lost control of the spin. As he pirouetted to the right, his left welly pirouetted right across the hall into the midst of some girls who were by now hysterical with laughter. Basher finally collapsed in a heap on the floor, exhausted. Melanie took a dainty bow and Basher eventually joined her. They made their exit to a tremendous round of applause.

David knew it was going to be difficult to follow an act like that, but he was aware that time was passing all too quickly. After some more dancing, Jimmy took the microphone and told some of his favourite jokes, while trying to hold on to a mischievous moustache. David wasn't at all sure whether they were laughing at Jimmy's jokes or his moustache.

After a break for refreshments Rosie took the microphone and sang one of her favourite songs entitled, 'When You're Young'. As she sang every line with feeling, David watched her expressions. He thought how beautiful she looked, with her dark curly hair shining in the lights of the disco stand. Rosie was aware of David's gaze and felt a flush of excitement, as she sang the song that could have been written for her.... with David in mind. The more David watched her the more he knew he was falling in love; but how could he tell her? He had wanted to tell her how lovely she looked tonight, but he just felt tongue-tied, unable to say a word. Maybe he feared the possibility of being rejected. He couldn't bear it if Rosie rejected his feelings for her: it would hurt far too much. Even at eleven.... praying for twelve, unrequited love could hurt deeply. One thought made him tingle all over and that was, that he felt sure Rosie had the same feelings for him.

The evening ended all too soon, with calls of, "It's too early!" and "Can't we have some more dancing?" However, David had to be firm, remembering Mr Mason's words - "Be sure you are locked up by eleven." Reluctantly, everyone gathered their belongings and asked when the next disco was to be: to David this was a good sign that they had enjoyed themselves. He didn't know, of course, but promised that they would hold another if they had not made enough to reach their target of one thousand pounds.

What they didn't know was that Tom would have been given a replacement dog anyway, in time.

David, Claire and friends stayed behind to clear up, as the rest left to join parents waiting for them outside the school gate. Little Tim, who had been delegated to collect all the paper plates and cups, called across the room to Basher who was stacking the chairs, "Hey, Basher, I didn't know you could ballet dance."

"Nor did I," said a smiling Basher.

"I can just see you dodging the dying swan," shouted Little Tim.

Jimmy couldn't help butting in, "You mean a dying hippo."

Basher bristled at Jimmy's remark. "You can't talk Lucas, your jokes were a bit crummy." Jimmy puffed his cheeks at the sheer audacity of Basher.

Then Rosie interjected as she wiped the tables down, "I thought he told a few crackers."

Jimmy saw the funny side of this and said, "Yes, that's where I got them from.... a few crackers." The tension that was building up between Jimmy and Basher was released as everyone laughed. It was not long before everything was cleared up and the hall returned to normal.

David had done a quick calculation of the evening's takings, while this was going on, and was disappointed to find that they were still short of their target.

As Melanie put on her coat she asked if anyone had seen Tom and, if so, how was he.

David explained, "My mother suggested that he see a clairvoyant, and has made an appointment for him for tomorrow." David then found himself having to explain what a clairvoyant was to an inquisitive Jimmy.

"Sounds a bit creepy to me," said Jimmy, shivering at the thought.

"What if Bella's been dognapped?" asked Little Tim, amazed that no one had thought of it before.

"Don't be a dumbo, McCreadie," scoffed Basher. "If Bella had been dognapped, don't you think someone would have had a ransom note by now?"

Little Tim looked as if his friend, Basher, had dealt him a body blow. "Oh," he sighed wearily, "I suppose so."

Once David had finished bagging all the money safely, he looked around the hall to make sure all was safe for the night. Jimmy had helped pack away the disco equipment in a corner until the next day, and David could see at a glance that all the sockets were safely out. "Come on," he said jokingly, "if we don't get a move on they'll be sending out a search party for us."

Jimmy looked directly at Basher as he said, "Yes, I can just see the headlines," mimicking a street corner news vendor, "MISSING! A DANCING HIPPO!" Basher threw his coat over his shoulder and chased Jimmy Lucas out of the hall and across the playground.

David and Rosie smiled, as they watched Melanie and Little Tim go running after them.

As they locked the large doors for the night, Jimmy's laugh could be heard right across the school grounds, with the sounds of Basher in hot pursuit, shouting, "Take that back Lucas!"

They walked slowly towards their high-spirited friends and David reached for Rosie's hand as they passed through the shade of the school building. It was a brief magical moment. There was a hazy orange moon to add to the magic of first love, casting a spell over them. David thought, 'If only I could tell her how I feel' and 'Why am I so tongued-tied?' All he seemed able to do was to press Rosie's hand gently, as they walked. All too soon the magic was broken, and he let go of her hand as they walked into the glare of the lamplight in the playground, and their waiting parents.

CHAPTER TEN: I STILL HAVE AN ACE UP MY SLEEVE

Tom sat nervously at the small round table in the middle of the room. Madame Francesca's flat was above an antiques shop in the High Street. He sat alone, as she had briefly left the room to answer the telephone in the hall.

Tom felt his nose twitch at the musty smell of old books and Eau de Cologne. Marion Jeffries had given him a brief idea of what to expect. However, Madame Francesca's voice and movements told him she was elderly, perhaps slightly plump, but with a very homely personality.

Although she had advertised under the name of Madame Francesca for many years, she was not like many of the more commercial clairvoyants, with all the trappings of their trade. Her parlour was the lounge of her flat and she owned the antique shop downstairs. She had had to give up running it some years earlier because of arthritis in her spine: it had been leased to someone else.

The silence in the room was in total contrast to the noise of the traffic in the street below. As he waited, Tom felt his stomach turn over and over. Had he done the right thing in coming? Would he feel even worse if his hopes were dashed against the rocks of disappointment? What if Madame Francesca told him Bella was dead? A cold chill ran through his heart. He felt like running.... out of the room, down the stairs and into the street.

However, as he reasoned with his torment, Madame Francesca's voice broke his thoughts. "I'm sorry to keep you waiting, Mr Sinclair."

Tom heard the door close quietly behind her, "That's quite all right," he said, feeling for the white stick he had placed beside his chair. How he loathed having to use a white stick again.... for all the help it gave him. It reminded him of his early days of blindness, before he knew the joy of owning a guide dog.

"The telephone is a great asset," said Madame Francesca resignedly, "but it can be most inconvenient at times." She laughed lightly as she pulled a chair out from the table and sat down opposite Tom. "Don't worry" she said in a low voice "I have taken it off the hook so that we wont be disturbed again."

Tom smiled to hide his nervousness, as Madame Francesca suddenly remembered she had left a small window open and closed it against the noise of the traffic below. The room was now tranquil, apart from the rattle and jangle of her beads and bracelets. Tom found the heavy scent of cologne almost too much as she prepared the table in readiness. "Now, dearie," she said, in a sympathetic tone, "what can I do to help you?"

Tom cleared his throat, then squeezed his hands together, before plucking up courage to ask the clairvoyant for help. "Madam Francesca," he said at last, struggling to find the right words, "what I've really come for is to ask if you could help me find my guide dog, Bella." Tom wrung his hands nervously. It wasn't easy for him, if he was honest with himself he had to admit that he never really believed in such things. "She's been missing for nearly two weeks now and I have heard that in your capacity.... as a medium, you have had some degree of success in finding missing persons." There was a long pause while the clairvoyant thought about it. "Well, yes, dearie, I suppose that is true. I have had some success in finding people who have gone missing." She spoke with a slightly husky voice which Tom found somewhat comforting. "However," she said, with a smile in her voice, "this is the first time I have been asked to find a missing dog."

Tom put his two hands firmly on the oak table in front of him, "But, Madame Francesca," he stressed, "you must understand, Bella is no ordinary dog." The blind man could feel the adrenalin pumping round his body now as his passionate plea came to the surface. "She has been personally responsible for raising thousands of pounds for the Guide Dog Association. She's met Royalty... and she's famous in her own right, but more than that," Tom paused for a moment, "much more than that.... she is my world. Without Bella," he said softly, "I am nothing."

Madame Francesca studied Tom as he spoke. "She sounds like a remarkable dog," she said compassionately.

"Oh, she is.... she really is," said Tom, who then reached for a newspaper cutting from the top pocket of his jacket. "Here, this will tell you all about her." He handed the neatly folded newspaper cutting to Madame Francesca, who promptly put on her reading glasses.

"Oh yes," she said, as a light went on in her memory, "now I remember, this is the story that has been in all the newspapers lately. Hmm!" she said as she continued to read, "she certainly looks a lovely dog."

Tom was quick to add, "Oh she is, everyone loves Bella. She's.... she's a very special dog." He heard Madame Francesca fold the newspaper cutting. "That's why," he said, raising his hand in the air, "I can't understand why no one has seen her. It's a complete mystery. If you ask me," he said in a subdued voice, "someone has found her and taken her in not knowing she's a blind person's eyes. Please!" he begged, "You must help me find her."

Madame Francesca was in no doubt that Tom was sincere. "She obviously means a great deal to you, Mr Sinclair," she said as she handed back the cutting.

"She's my whole life!" cried Tom.

"All right then," said Madame Francesca, as she pulled her chair up closer to the table, "I'll see what I can do.... but, I can't promise anything." Then she added, "Mind you, some dogs are known to have telepathic powers."

Tom was quick to give credence to this. "If any dog ever had telepathic powers, it's Bella," he said, with a hint of nervous excitement, "she could read my mind."

"Well, let's give it a try," said the clairvoyant, as she reached across the table. "Right then, dearie, what I want you to do is grip my hands across the table...." Tom put both his hands out slowly and Madame Francesca took hold of them gently. She knew how nervous he was and she tried to make it easier for him. "That's right. Now grip tight.... then relax. That's better!" she said, once she had removed the tremor in Tom's hands. Now try to relax completely.... relax.... just relax," she said in a hushed voice. Tom felt his nervousness suddenly subside in the quiet of the room, with only the muted sounds of life in the street below. Madame Francesca closed her eyes and tried to concentrate all her powers on a mental picture of Bella. "I want you to imagine it's a gloriously sunny day," she said softly to Tom. "You are in the park with Bella at your side and you can hear the birds singing in the trees.... a church bell ringing in the distance, and you can feel the warm kiss of the sun on your cheeks. You feel totally at peace with the world.... and oh so relaxed."

Tom was actually there in his mind.... with Bella; it was a wonderful feeling.

"Are you relaxed," asked Madame Francesca.

"Yes," said Tom lazily. In a curious way his nervous tension had vanished, and had been replaced with a mixture of excited anticipation.

"Good!" said the clairvoyant, pleased to know Tom was responding to her relaxation technique. "Now," she said, in a very precise manner with her eyes closed, "I want you to transmit.... across to me, all the love you feel for Bella. Let me feel the bond between you." This was easy for Tom. "Yes, yes, that's it." Madame Francesca was gripping Tom's hands very tightly now. "I can feel it.... it's strong.... very strong," she said in a low, serious, voice. For the first time Tom sensed emotion in her words. "Wait!" she said excitedly. "I think I am getting something." Tom felt himself tense with the urgency in her voice.

"Oh please, God," he prayed inwardly, "let it be Bella.... let it be good news."

Madame Francesca gripped his hands even tighter. "Yes, I'm getting something." She shivered. "It's cold and dark and.... I can hear sounds.... like....?" She struggled to identify the sounds. "Like.... like running water. Yes! That's it.... running water. It sounds as if it's dripping.... but it's so dark."

A shiver ran up Tom's spine as he gripped the clairvoyant's hands repeatedly in an attempt to will her on.... he wanted to hear more.... so very much more. Madame Francesca spoke more slowly, more articulately as she continued, "There's.... a figure or a statue of some kind.... it appears to be broken. I can just make out the letter 'M'. She tightened her grip on Tom's hands so hard it hurt, but then she let go and just dropped her hands on the table, exhausted from her efforts. "It's no good," she sighed, "that's about all we're going to get I'm afraid."

Tom felt as though he was suspended in an agonising limbo. "But, is she alive?" he begged desperately: he had gone this far and he wasn't going to be left in mid-air.

The clairvoyant shook her head wearily. "I don't know," she said, "it's hard to tell."

Tom tried to make sense of the jumbled words, "A broken statue with the letter 'M'," he said vaguely. "It's not much to go on is it?"

Madame Francesca leaned back in her chair and stretched to try to ease the muscle tension in her neck and shoulders. "Well," she said, "I did warn you that I couldn't promise very much." Tom's heart sank and he sat motionless, wondering if the whole thing had been a failure. Madame Francesca was acutely aware of his desperate need to find his beloved Bella.

"We could, of course, try the cards," she offered. "You never know, they might just come up trumps." Tom's face lit up: he knew he was clutching at straws.... but, anything was worth a try.... anything.

"Yes, yes please!" he said painfully, "if you think it might help."

Madame Francesca moved over to the sideboard and took out a pack of playing cards, then resumed her seated position at the table. "Right! Now dearie, what I want you to do is...." Madame Francesca spoke slowly so that Tom could get a clear mental picture of what she was about to do. "I'm going to spread the cards out in a circle, in front of you, and what I want you to do is select one card for me from anywhere in the circle." She took hold of Tom's arm and traced an outline of the circle of cards for him, with his hand. "I have placed the cards face down and when you are ready, I want you to select any one card. Have you got that?" Tom nodded nervously. "Then hand it to me and we will see what you come up with."

Tom carefully selected a card from the circle and handed it to Madame Francesca, who looked at the card and sighed. "Hmm! The King of Hearts.... he represents the King of Heartbreak. This means," she said thoughtfully, "that you have suffered a great deal of heartbreak.... and shed too many tears of late."

Tom nodded. "It's true," he agreed, "very true."

Madame Francesca asked Tom to choose another card. His hand hovered over the circle before he chose the next card. "Ah!" she said, "The Jack of Spades.... the knave; he's nobody's fool. He represents an obstacle blocking the way of progress." She sighed once more. "Not much help to us I'm afraid." Tom felt his spirits sinking as he selected another card. "Oh dear," she frowned, "The Queen of Clubs.... a black queen. I'm afraid she shines no light for us at all" Madame Francesca knew it was pointless continuing. "As far as I can see, dear, it's not worth going on. The cards appear to be stacked against you." Tom felt tears of frustration welling up into his unseeing eyes.

"Lady Luck isn't exactly being helpful, is she?" It was more of a rhetorical question really.

"Well, I'm not going to give up.... not while there is a chance of finding Bella." said Tom, stoically.

Madame Francesca felt helpless to assist this poor blind man in his suffering. She had been unable to make head or tail of the jumble of words that had come through to her. She looked across the table at Tom and saw the pain visibly etched on his tired face. "I really wish there was something more I could do to help you, Mr Sinclair. You never know though, you might just go home and something falls into place, making sense of what I have told you...." She whispered, "Stranger things have happened."

Tom thanked Madame Francesca for at least trying to help. He added, 'The cards might have been stacked against me, but...." he reached defiantly for a card in the circle on the table and declared, ".... I still have an ace up my sleeve." He tossed the card down on the table again, knowing that the ace up his sleeve was 'Love' and he knew love could move mountains.

Madame Francesca was astonished as she retrieved the card Tom had just thrown back down on the table. It was the Ace of Hearts, but.... how could he have known? Her first instinct was to tell him. However, she decided not to, as he had been through enough for one day. However, she couldn't help feeling strangely optimistic at this turn of the cards. In fact, she couldn't have told him where the Ace of Hearts was, as she had dealt them face-down from the pack, and yet it tied in with his thought pattern. She then dismissed the whole thing as pure coincidence.

Tom thanked her for her time and asked how much he owed her. "Oh that's all right," she said smiling, "I don't want any money."

Tom took his wallet from his pocket, "But you must! You've given me your valuable time."

Madame Francesca put a hand on his wallet, in an attempt to close it for him, "And how many hours have you given free.... and for many years too?" What could Tom say to that?

"Well, that is most kind of you, Madame Francesca," said Tom gratefully.

"I just hope you get some good news soon," said the clairvoyant. She saw him safely out of the flat, down the stairs, and into the street where they said their goodbyes.

It took Tom a minute or two to get his bearings - he was so used to Bella guiding him. He twitched his nose for identifiable smells, to give him direction. Suddenly, he heard a familiar voice call out to him. It was David, who had managed to skip the football game at school, and Claire was with him, having feigned not feeling well. David was about to ask Tom how he had got on with Madame Francesca when he saw a familiar figure running towards him.... with a pretty girl. His heart skipped a beat as he realised it was Rosie and Jimmy Lucas. Claire had seen them too. "Well, look who it isn't?" she said with a hint of sarcasm. "It's Jimmy, and Rosie too."

Tom was pleased to know that he had such an entourage to escort him home. An out of breath Jimmy said "Hello!" to Tom and asked what David was starting to ask - how had Tom got on with Madame Francesca.

"Well," Tom began, but wasn't quite sure where to start or even if it would make sense to any of them, "I'm afraid she wasn't able to help very much at all." He could almost hear the disappointment on their faces. "All she could tell me was about a broken statue.... with the letter 'M', and that there was running or dripping water." He sighed, "And that it was cold and dark. I'm afraid it didn't make much sense to me at all."

The children looked at each other, puzzled expressions on their faces. "A statue with the letter 'M'?" said David shaking his head. "Sounds a bit strange to me." However, Claire had an idea as she guided Tom towards the safe side of the pavement; out of the way of pedestrians.

"Why don't we think of some names beginning with the letter 'M'?" Between them they came up with names like Mandy, Mark, Melisa, Melanie, Margaret, Michael, Mary, Maria.....

"Wait!" cried David to Rosie, who had just offered the last two names. "What were those last two names?"

Rosie looked slightly bewildered at David's reaction. "Mary.... and Maria," she said slowly.

A smile broke out on David's face. "That's it! Mary and Maria! The Madonna!" He said excitedly, "That could be it!"

Jimmy was quick to dampen everyone's spirits. "But that could only be found in a church," he said mockingly, "and it would hardly be dark and wet in a church."

However, David's brain was working overtime again, and he said, "Not if it was an old ruin." Tom suddenly felt lighter in spirit and, yet, he was afraid to raise his hopes too high.

Rosie smiled as a thought filtered through her mind, "I've just remembered!" she said, absentmindedly wrapping her woollen scarf around her neck, "there's an old ruined church about a mile from town. I remember seeing it from the bus when I was going to a friend's house." There was a stunned silence as everyone digested the possibilities that were now almost too exciting to contemplate.

David was the first to speak out. "A statue.... broken, with the letter 'M'; running or dripping water; cold and dark."

He hit his fist into his hand as he turned to face Tom. "Does this make any sense to you now, Tom?"

He answered cautiously, still not daring to raise his hopes too much. "Well, it does seem a possibility."

Jimmy asked Rosie, "How far did you say it was from town?"

"Only about a mile, that's all. It's on the outskirts of town."

Claire was too excited for words. "Well!" she said, "What are we waiting for?"

Jimmy Lucas couldn't resist the temptation, "I'm game!" he said laughing, "I've always wanted to go on a wild goose chase."

"How long would it take us to get there?" asked Rosie.

David frowned as he tried to calculate. "Let's see," he said, tossing his blond hair out of his eyes, "a mile or a mile and a half.... I would say about forty-five minutes." He looked at his watch. "Half-past-three," he stated. He then asked Tom, even though he was well aware that this could be yet another false alarm. "Do you feel like walking, Tom?"

Their blind friend turned up his collar against the cold wind and said without hesitation, "Just you try and stop me."

"Great!" said the children, laughing at Tom's choice of words. David offered Tom his arm, saying "We can be there before it gets dark." Jimmy decided they might need a strong torch and decided that as his house was the nearest, he would call in for his father's torch from the garage. Everyone agreed this was a sensible thing to do.

As they all walked briskly down the High Street, Tom was aware of the aroma of coffee, coming from Giovanni's, and his heart ached.... ached for Bella. Please God, he thought desperately, let this all make sense. He walked briskly holding onto David's arm, on past Giovanni's, towards the outskirts of the town.... and into the unknown.

CHAPTER ELEVEN: DO YOU BELIEVE IN MIRACLES?

The headlights of the oncoming cars cut through the late afternoon mist which increased in density as Tom, David, Claire, Rosie and Jimmy walked to the outskirts of town.

"How much farther is it?" asked Jimmy impatiently, kicking at a stray stone in the middle of the pavement.

"It can't be much farther," said Rosie, half afraid she had made a mistake in her judgement of the distance.

David was concerned for Tom and asked, "Do you want to rest for a while, Tom?"

He was quick to assure David that he was fine and couldn't stop now, not while there was even a flicker of hope ahead. The urban pavements ceased and they found themselves on a rural road where they had to be extra careful, keeping well in to the side of the road.

"Are you sure this is the right road, Rosie?" asked David, after walking what felt like a marathon.

"I think so," said Rosie. Then she stopped suddenly, with confusion written all over her pretty face.

"Oh David!" she said, cupping her hands over her mouth, "I've just realised, the bus may have gone along the other route.... and not this one." Jimmy shook his fist in silent anger while Claire sighed heavily. David, too, couldn't help showing his disappointment. Tom just held his breath.... hoping. "I'm sorry," said Rosie, tearfully, "I really am."

Tom knew she had only tried to help and reassured her, "It's all right, love, don't worry, we'll find it."

"Well!" said David, wearily, "we'll just have to try the other route tomorrow, that's all" Tom felt his heart sink.

A wave of disappointment crashed down on his heart but he could not let the children see how he felt. "There's always tomorrow," he said philosophically. David was suddenly acutely aware of how awful Rosie must be feeling.

"Don't worry, Rosie," he said, putting a comforting hand

on her arm. "It will be dark soon, so.... maybe it's just as well."

Jimmy and Claire meanwhile had decided to check at least beyond the bend in the road up ahead of them, just in case. David was about to shout after them, when Jimmy and Claire stopped in their tracks. "There it is!" shouted Jimmy, excitedly.

Claire added, "You were right after all, Rosie."

Everyone cheered loudly and David took Tom by the arm. David felt like kissing Rosie, but he realised this was just not the time or the place. "Come on, Rosie," he called, "Let's hurry." Tom couldn't believe this was happening to him. Never had he experienced such highs and lows in his spirits in any one day and, for a brief moment, he wondered if his poor heart could take it.

Now there was an urgency in everyone's pace as they walked the short distance. David called to Jimmy and Claire to keep well into the side of the road as the oncoming cars were travelling fast. The hedgerow hampered their vision until they reached the final bend in the road. Suddenly.... there it was. Giant Gothic arches, that had once framed stained glass windows, now loomed eerily through the swirling mist. It was situated at the far end of a field, surrounded by meadowland.

David noticed a light coming from a farmhouse, about a quarter of a mile farther down the road. He felt relieved to know that at least there was some sign of civilisation around. The daylight was fading fast and they would have to act quickly. He was also aware of the fact that no one.... not even Jimmy's parents knew where they were. It had been a spontaneous decision in all the excitement and they just hadn't thought to tell anyone. Well, they were here now and David knew that he would be held responsible if anything went wrong. Even so, he tried to be positive in his thinking as he described the scene ahead of them to Tom.

Jimmy turned into the field, holding open the gate until each of them was through. As they came face to face with the ruins, each wondered if Madame Francesca's message would have any meaning at all. David and Jimmy decided to go forward to reconnoitre the ruins.... for safety reasons. The girls stayed with Tom who was feeling decidedly nervous about the whole idea. The two boys returned in no time at all. David said, with an air of confidence, that it was reasonably safe for them to go inside. However, he briefed everyone on the need to be vigilant since there was a lot of crumbling masonry around.

Cautiously they entered the ruin. Tom held tightly onto David's arm, followed closely by Claire and Rosie. Jimmy lead the way with his torch picking out the safest route, step by step. He was glad now that he had borrowed his dad's powerful flashlight. The ebbing daylight and the swirling mist gave everyone an eerie feeling, as they entered the skeleton of the church. Jimmy's torchlight casting furtive shadows against the monumental walls that now surrounded them, didn't help. Rosie couldn't help thinking that it was like a scene from a horror film. She shuddered at the thought. There was a strange silence as each one of them was wrapped up in their own thoughts and fears.

Suddenly, Rosie let out a piercing scream. Jimmy spun around immediately, shining his torch on Rosie, who was shielding her face with her arms. Trapped for a split second, caught in Jimmy's torchlight, was a bat, homing in on a crevice, high up on the wall above them.

"It's all right Rosie," shouted David, "it's only a bat." Claire and Jimmy breathed a sigh of relief as Tom explained to them that bats are harmless to humans. He said that being scared of them was a myth that had built up out of the use of bats in horror films. Even so, Rosie took some convincing. They continued to creep forward step by step into the ruins.

"I must admit," said Claire in a whisper, "it is a bit scary in here," as she scanned the air for more bats.

"I wonder if it's haunted?" said Jimmy, not really wanting to find out.

"I don't know, but I bet it was a lovely church once."

Jimmy laughed, "Yes, but I doubt if they get many people at Sunday service these days"

"Jimmy!" shouted Claire, in a hushed voice, "Where's your respect? This is still a house of God."

"A house of God?" cried Jimmy, in his high pitched voice. "What! This old ruin?"

"Be quiet!" shushed Claire, "or he'll hear you."

Jimmy sounded indignant as he replied, "Well! He didn't hear me when I asked him to help find Bella, did he?"

David found the banter between Jimmy and Claire annoying. "Be quiet, you two!" There was silence once more but now the silence was even more eerie. It was cold and getting darker by the minute and the swirling mist didn't make it any easier for them to find their way. David was beginning to think that Jimmy was right; that it might well be a wild goose chase. Tom was also silent, but all his other senses were on full alert and he was concentrating all his energies on conjuring a mental picture from these sources.

They slowly made their way to what would have once been the sanctuary, where they found the ground to be more solid. Now they could all relax a little knowing that the ground wasn't going to cave in under them. Jimmy shone the torch up at the large Gothic arches, where he could see the carved angels with broken wings.... still praying.

"Look!" said David, taking command of the situation, "I'll stay here with Tom, while you, Jimmy...." he paused briefly, "....and the girls too, have a look around outside the church on this side." He sighed, "There's no sign of the Madonna in here."

Jimmy retorted, "If there isn't one in here, then I doubt very much if we'll find one outside the church."

David sounded irritated as he replied, "Well, have a look anyway."

Rosie made the first move. "Come on Jimmy, we can have a look, just in case."

Jimmy tutted but reluctantly went with the girls,

shining his torch for them to see their way. David stayed put with Tom, for now they had no light but he shouted after them, "Make sure you all stay together, and be careful" he stressed, "the structure is none too safe." Jimmy rolled his eyes skyward as David again shouted after them not to touch anything. However, he knew David had good reason to be so cautious and, in a strange way, Jimmy respected him.

As the voices of the others faded into the mist, Tom turned his collar up higher against the cold wind whistling through the gaps in the walls of the old ruin. He rubbed his hands to get the circulation going again as David sighed wearily. "Well, there's no sign of Bella here, Tom." He looked at the brave blind man and paused before saying what he must. "Do you think Madame Francesca could be wrong?"

Tom gave a sorrowful sigh and then leaned with both hands on his white stick. "I don't know, David," he said resignedly, "I suppose I was expecting a miracle." David looked up at the outline of the huge Gothic arches that loomed threateningly above them. "Do you believe in miracles?" he said softly: for the first time he had time to feel a little scared.

"I wish I did, David." said Tom. David couldn't help wondering if Tom had been born blind or if he was blinded by accident. There was an uneasy silence as David struggled to find the right words, hoping not to offend.

"I hope you don't mind my asking, Tom, but have you always been blind?"

Tom smiled at David's direct question. "No! of course, I don't mind you asking, and no" he added, "I haven't always been blind. It was due to an accident that happened a long time ago."

He took a deep breath before continuing, "They had told me there was nothing they could do. Apparently," explained, "I had a disease in the retina of the eye. It was, of course, very hard to accept. I was still young, with my whole life ahead of me and I grew angry" he said, reflecting on the futility of such an emotion, "angry with myself and angry with the whole world, I remember," he said, looking straight ahead into the darkness. Tom was aware that he was baring his soul, probably for the first time in a very long time. It somehow didn't seem to matter that David was so young in years, or that they were in the midst of a damp, cold and eerie old church ruin. On the contrary, it felt strangely spiritual. He felt emotions surfacing that had been buried for a long time, and yet, he had no desire to suppress them. A feeling of inner calm swept over him, engulfing his entire being. He realised, for the first time, that you have to face the darkness before you can see the light.

David could see that his friend was lost in a world of his own and didn't want to intrude further. They were silent for a while until, suddenly, Tom cleared his throat, "Of course," he said, straightening himself up, "I then realised how stupid and selfish I had been. I began to rationalise the whole thing." He said, philosophically, "I told myself I was lucky.... I had my memories, whereas many blind people had never been able to see, those that had been born blind."

David was fascinated and for a moment he had forgotten his fears. "And so," said Tom, with a shrug of his shoulders, "I was given a white stick and, for many years, I coped the best way I could." He smiled at the memory "Then someone suggested that I apply for a guide dog.... that's when Bella came into my life, that's when I began to live again, and I've never looked back since." He took another deep breath before going on. "Bella is the best thing that ever happened to me," he said. "She taught me to live again, and to be a free spirit. She gave me back my independence and that," he said softly, his unseeing eyes searching the darkness, "meant so very much to me. I was so grateful for my new-found freedom that I wanted others who were blind, to know that the eyes of a guide dog can transform life." He paused for a moment to reflect on his philosophy of life. "That's why I decided to devote my whole life, along with

Bella, to raising funds for the Guide Dogs for the Blind Association." David saw Tom's eyes mist over as he concluded, "We were a great team.... together." He swallowed hard in an effort to move the lump in his throat. Then, in frustrated anger he banged his white stick on the ground, "Bella! Oh Bella!" he cried. "Where are you?" his plaintive voice trailed off in the mist. David had great difficulty holding back his own tears, but felt he had to be strong for Tom.

"Don't worry Tom," said David, with more compassion than was usual for a boy of his age. "We'll soon get you another guide dog, and then...." he said with enthusiasm, "you can continue with your charity work." David didn't know what else to say to make Tom feel any easier. He couldn't tell him about the Autumn Fayre and the school disco, not yet anyway. There was an uneasy silence as they both strayed into own private thoughts.

Suddenly, Tom gave a jerk that almost frightened David. "What was that?" he whispered.

David diffused the moment quickly, saying "Oh I expect it's Jimmy and the girls coming back."

"No! No!" said Tom anxiously. The one thing about being blind is that your hearing is so much keener than the average person's.

They both held their breath for a minute to listen hard. All they could hear was the wind whistling through the gaps in the massive stone walls where doors used to be, and the faint sound of the traffic from the distant road. However, they were interrupted by the sound of Jimmy and the girls making their way back to the sanctuary.

"Well," said Jimmy, puffing and panting as he reached Tom and David, "there's no sign of anything out there." The two girls confirmed this.

"Be quiet a minute!" whispered David, "Tom thinks he can hear something."

"Like what?" Jimmy asked quizzically.

Tom raised a hand in the air, "Shhhhhh!" he begged.

The children watched Tom prodding around with his white stick. He moved across to the other side of the sanctuary, still prodding and poking, with David close behind him. "David?" he called, "Come here, quickly!" He pointed to a pile of rubble at his feet, then knelt down to feel it. Rosie and Claire looked on in amazement as they watched their blind friend start to pull away some of the stones. David was at his side, kneeling with him; he didn't know what Tom was hoping to find, but knew whatever it was he was serious. Tom began to pull away the stones feverishly and then in a breathless voice, asked, "Tell me David.... is this the Madonna?" David couldn't believe his eyes. He quickly took over where Tom had left off, until he found the smooth outline of what was.... a statue of the Madonna. Jimmy was speechless as he shone the torch for David to get a closer look.

"It is!" shouted David excitedly. "It's the Madonna." Rosie hugged him as he added.... "or it was the Madonna."

Tom's senses were on full alert once again. "Listen!" he shouted above the excitement. "Can you hear it? It's getting nearer." David, Jimmy and the girls listened hard, but they still couldn't hear a thing. "It's coming from underground," shouted Tom excitedly. There was no stopping Tom now. "It's.... it's a.... whining sound!" he said, almost beside himself. "It's Bella, it has to be." David and his friends stood in silence. "Quick!" shouted Tom, "See if there's a trapdoor or an opening of some kind." There was an urgency in his voice as he added, "there has to be one.... somewhere."

Rosie and Claire stood beside Tom with bated breath, while David and Jimmy searched the area. "There doesn't seem to be one," said Jimmy disappointedly.

"But there has to be one somewhere," shouted Tom. He knew there was no going back now, not now he had come this far, and if those sounds were Bella, there was no way he could leave without finding his way to her. He listened hard once more for the sounds that he had heard earlier. Then he was sure, as he heard it again. He followed the sound until he found the loudest point, which was directly over the broken pieces of the Madonna. "David!" he called, with a new excitement in his voice. "Come and look here, quickly. See if there's a trapdoor of some kind here." David and Jimmy, pulled frantically at the stones and rubble, while Tom and the girls silently prayed. Suddenly, as David and Jimmy heaved a huge piece of the broken statue to one side, David shouted, "Look! It's a trapdoor!"

"I only hope we can get it open," said Jimmy excitedly. Tom thanked God quietly as the two boys heaved at the pull ring on the trapdoor, but it was proving to be more difficult than they had envisaged.

"If only we had a piece of rope," sighed David. Tom had Bella's lead in his pocket (since she had gone missing he had never ventured outside without it, just in case) and he now offered it to the boys. Tom and the girls joined in to give an almighty tug and finally managed to get the door wide open.

Once everyone had got their breath back, Jimmy shone his torch down into the black hole, lighting a dozen or more stone steps. "This must lead down into the crypt," he said in a hushed voice. David peered down into the hole and Rosie put her arm around him to peer over his shoulder. Claire too wasn't going to miss out.

"What a musty smell," she said, holding her nose. Tom tried hard to identify any smell other than that of the dank smell that comes from centuries of decay, but it was difficult. The blanket of mist merely wrapped up any chance of identifying any individual smells.

"Shhh!" whispered David, trying to see if they could hear anything.

"There!" shouted Rosie, "Did you hear it?" David did and was now determined. If it was Bella down there, they were going to have to find a way to get her out. He looked at the broken steps, but there was no time to think of himself.

"Can you shine the torch down the steps for me, Jimmy.... I'm going down."

"Can I come with you?" begged Jimmy.

"No!" said David, in a serious voice. "For one thing there's only enough room for one, by the look of it. And for another...." he paused, "....and for another, if anything should happen, at least you'll be able to get Tom and the girls safely back home." Jimmy had to admit that it made sense.

David began to climb down into the unknown. Rosie looked around at the darkness and the old ruins and a chill ran through her body. "Please be careful, David," she said, wrapping her scarf even tighter round her chin.

Tom could only stand by helplessly. "Yes, be careful, David," he said, echoing Rosie's sentiment. David finally disappeared below the trapdoor. There was silence for a moment or two, then to Rosie's horror there was the sound of rumbling stones that ended with a crash and a thud. Tom, Rosie, Claire and Jimmy held their breath.... not daring to speak.

"David!" shouted Jimmy, "David! Are you all right?" Tom and the girls began breathing again as David answered in a slightly injured tone.

"I think.... so!" Jimmy tried to pierce the darkness with his torch but couldn't see his friend.

"What happened?" he shouted down into the darkness. There was an agonising silence, until David heard Rosie beg him to say if he was hurt.

Jimmy couldn't wait any longer, "I'm going in after him," he said frantically.

"No!" begged Tom. "No! Jimmy, not yet anyway."

They heard a moan, then movement, as David tried to get his thoughts together. "I'm OK," he said faintly, and everyone breathed a sigh of relief. "I must have fallen on a broken step," he said, still somewhat dazed. David realised that he must have hit his head and been stunned for a minute or two. Then he tried to get up.... but he felt a surge of pain as he tried to put weight on his twisted ankle. He winced as he tried to walk, but one way or another he was going to walk. He couldn't tell them about his ankle. He shouted for Jimmy to throw down the torch as he couldn't see a thing in the darkness of the crypt. Jimmy carefully threw down the torch, heard it land with a thud and David retrieved it. Rosie begged him to be careful; she'd had enough frights for one day.

David ventured further into the crypt, hobbling painfully on his ankle. He had to push his way through centuries of cobwebs that now looked like his mother's net curtains in the kitchen. The mist had laced them all with dew and interwoven them into a beautiful, although somewhat ghostly, fabric of time. He peered into the first chamber of the crypt, shining the torch around but there was nothing. He continued doing this in each of the chambers but began to think it must have been Tom's imagination after all. He found a gap in the outer wall and rested beside it so that he could inhale a lung full of clean air.

His ankle was throbbing and he could feel the swelling above his shoe and didn't quite know how he was going to climb back up the steps. What was more important, however, was how was he going to tell Tom and the others that it had been a false alarm. He decided he had no option but to make his way back to the steps and tell them. Still wincing with pain, he managed to make his way back slowly.

Suddenly he stopped, he felt sure he heard a sound coming from the middle chamber, but he knew he had covered that in his search. He decided it must be a rat or something and began to walk away. Then he heard it again. He shone his torch through the mist lighting up the musty chamber. He could see something that looked like a concealed entrance that would lead to one of the other chambers. On closer inspection David could see that it was concealed by centuries of cobwebs and dust. There was a small gap in the centre of the tunnel, where David shone his torch. He peered in through the gap and his heart missed a beat.... There he saw two very frightened but loving eyes, and a weak whimper greeted him. In that moment, David was oblivious of any pain in his ankle. His eyes were filled with tears at the sheer joy of finding Bella alive.

"Bella!" he screeched. "Bella! Oh Bella!" Bella recognised his voice and began clawing her way through to him with excited whimpers. David had to tell the others and he shouted at the top of his voice, "IT'S BELLA.... AND SHE'S ALIVE." Tom dropped to his knees to thank God. This surely was a miracle, he thought. Jimmy, Claire and Rosie hugged each other, hardly able to believe the news.

"Is she all right?" shouted Tom, who was close to tears.

"Yes! She seems to be," answered David. His voice was beginning to get hoarse from all the shouting.

"Do you want any help?" bellowed Jimmy. David assured him he would soon shout if he did. David decided he would try to locate the other side of the tunnel, as he reasoned that Bella would have had to find a way in there somehow.

"It's all right, Bella," he said softly, "we'll soon have you out of there." He hobbled as quickly as the pain in his ankle would allow into the next chamber where he was sure Bella must have got into the wall cavity. He saw what looked like a pile of debris pouring out of the wall. He moved in closer with the torch and heard Bella crying with excitement. This was it, though it amazed David to think how Bella must have got in there; it was such a small hole. He could only assume that she had heard voices above the crypt and she had tried to follow the sound, clawing her way into the cavity. He suddenly realised he was going to need something with which to hold on to Bella and remembered the lead they had used to lift the trapdoor.

He again made his way back to the bottom of the steps and asked Jimmy to throw down the lead. How he cursed his swollen ankle, it was slowing him up very much but he still didn't tell the others. He eventually managed to pull some of the rubble away from the opening to the cavity but she was unable to turn round in the confined space.

David talked gently to Bella reassuring her that he was going to get her out safely and then home, as he coaxed her to move backwards towards him. She was weak from lack of food but finally emerged free, she gave a cry of happiness. David hugged her. "Oh Bella! You don't know how glad I am to see you." He then quickly put the lead around her neck and through the loop, noose fashion. He couldn't risk losing her again after all the trouble it had taken to find her.

"Come on, girl!" he said, easing her slowly out of the chamber and into the dark passage to the steps. "I've someone waiting to see you." He felt Bella's weary tail flapping against his legs.

Tom was still down on his knees willing his beloved Bella not to have been harmed in any way and brought out safely to him.

Rosie was becoming anxious at the length of time it was taking David to bring Bella out. "It feels as though he's been down there for hours," she complained, "What's he doing?" Claire just bit her bottom lip in excited anticipation. Tom would have been the first to admit that he was never much of a one for praying, but he reckoned he had prayed more in the last twenty minutes than in the whole of his life.

Suddenly they saw a light coming from the darkness of the tunnel that lead to the steps. "Here they are!" shouted a jubilant Jimmy. He offered to help David with Bella on the crumbling steps.

"Thanks, Jimmy," said David. "It would be better if I threw the torch up to you, then you can shine it down the steps, then I'll have two hands free to help Bella up the steps. She's a bit weak."

"Be careful!" called Tom, who could hardly believe what was happening; that he would be reunited with Bella in the next few minutes. With David's help Bella began to climb the crumbling stone steps one at a time and finally emerged from the trapdoor followed by an exhausted David.

Bella was beside herself with joy as she recognised the children's voices, then she slipped right through their hugs and into Tom's waiting arms. "Oh Bella!" he cried, "My beautiful Bella!" In that moment they were lost in a world of their own, a world that only a blind person and their guide dog could truly experience and understand.

There was a sudden break in the dark clouds, allowing the moon to briefly illuminate the misty scene. It created a strangely beautiful sight in the midst of the old church ruins. The silvery shafts of moonlight burst through the large Gothic arches where the windows once had been, seeming to disperse the mist surrounding Tom and Bella, bathing them in silver light.

Jimmy, Claire, Rosie and David, who still sat on the trapdoor and the top of the steps, watched in wonder. It took Rosie's breath away; she could almost hear a choir of angels singing, "Hallelujah!" They were all close to tears. Claire felt goosepimples on her arms under her anorak and was the first to go to Tom and Bella; the others followed close behind.

Tom wiped the tears from his eyes as Bella, tired and weak as she was, again greeted the children with her happy tail. As they hugged and patted her, they found she was dusty but very much alive. David looked at a deliriously happy Tom and asked, "Now do you believe in miracles, Tom?"

Tom spoke softly through his tears, "I most certainly do, David," he said, looking towards heaven, "I certainly do."

Claire was amazed that Bella had survived for almost two weeks without food and water. However, David said that he did hear dripping water down in the crypt and Jimmy was quick to add, "That is what Madame Francesca said, wasn't it, Tom?" Tom agreed and Jimmy then added his own theory that Bella probably lived on field mice and insects that entered the crypt through the holes in the walls, from the fields around the ruins.

Tom hugged Bella again for the twentieth time. "Poor Bella!" he said, kissing the top of her head. "When she ran off frightened she must have wandered into the church ruins and found the trapdoor open." He kissed her again. "She wasn't to know that her movements would bring that crumbling statue of the Madonna down behind her, trapping her in the crypt." He held Bella close again with his face next to hers, saying, "But you're safe now, Bella. You're safe." His tears now flowed unashamedly, but this time they were tears of real joy and happiness, like happiness he had never known before. The children joined in his happiness with tears of their own.

David was the first to recover and looked at Jimmy, suggesting, "Well, I suppose we ought to be getting back. Our parents will be worried stiff by now." The girls agreed.

Tom couldn't wait to say, "Come on, Bella my love, we're going home." What a wonderful thought that was for Tom, after all the anguish he had endured over the last two weeks.

The silvery strands of moonlight began to fade, as they prepared to make their way out of the old ruins. Although the mist was now lifting, the moon had completely disappeared behind the heavy clouds and it was very dark. Jimmy shone his torch once more to lead everyone safely out of the church. Bella was tired from her excitement and more than a little weak from her imprisonment in the crypt, thus progress was slow.

Rosie suddenly noticed that David was limping. "David?" she enquired, "Are you hurt? You're limping." David passed it off as just a bit of a sprain, saying it would be all right. However, she offered her shoulder for support which he accepted, while Claire and Jimmy helped Tom and Bella back to the road. "You were so brave," said Rosie, "I was really proud of you." With praise like that from Rosie, David managed to make light of his injury and put up with the pain.

They made their way out onto the road and headed for

home. Tom suggested that they telephone their parents to explain where they were, but they were nearly back in the town before they found a telephone box. After a lot of excited explanations to their parents by telephone, the children accompanied Tom and Bella safely home.

CHAPTER TWELVE: LIKE ALL HAPPY TAILS

After a blissful night's sleep, Bella had completely revived and was playfully willing Tom to get up and out of bed as usual; there was so much they had both missed. Tom hugged her close to him and it felt so good, so very good. He had been afraid he would never have the joy of holding his black Labrador again but here she was. Now he knew there was a God, and he believed in miracles.

He was soon out of bed and opening the curtains that had remained closed for the past two weeks, and he felt the late November sun kiss his day 'Good Morning'! He smiled, taking a deep breath to expand his lungs. "It's good to be alive," he told himself as he felt the familiar draught from his beloved Bella's happy tail. She could read Tom's mind and right now her barometer of joy was on high. "Come on, girl!" he said, bending down to kiss her on her nose, "Let's go downstairs and get some breakfast while we have some peace and quiet."

It was eight-thirty as Tom and Bella made their way into the kitchen, where Tom put the kettle on for a cup of tea. Suddenly, the telephone rang, "It looks as though I spoke too soon," said Tom as he made his way through to the living room. It proved to be the first of many calls from TV and radio stations, newspaper reporters, and a host of well wishers.

News of the television cameras coming to film himself and Bella at home excited Tom enormously and Bella was as quick as ever to sense his mood. They were both almost too excited to eat the breakfast that Tom eventually found time to prepare; Bella had eaten her fill the night before anyway. The rest of the day was a haze of flash bulbs and stories told over and over to television and press reporters and to numerous callers. But, oh what joy!

By four-thirty, the afternoon mist was descending over the ebbing light of a sunny day. Melanie, Basher and Little

Tim made their way out of the school grounds and down towards the bus station. On their way they passed a newsagent's with large posters outside the shop. "Look!" said Melanie, unable to hide her joy. "It's all about Bella!" She read out, excitedly, the large print on the boards. "BELLA FOUND! SCHOOLBOY HAILED AS HERO!"

Little Tim smiled, "Everyone seems to be talking about Bella, don't they?"

"Yeah!" said Basher, throwing his school bag over his shoulder, "It will probably be on telly tonight." Melanie suggested that they call in at the newsagent's to buy a paper, then they could read the full story.

The three of them stood in the half-light of the newsagent's doorway as Basher read out aloud the good news story of Bella's return, with Melanie and Little Tim peering over his shoulder:

'Bella found alive and well! Schoolboy hailed as hero!'

Basher raised his eyes skyward at the sensationalism of the press before reading on....

'Yesterday, around 4pm eleven year old schoolboy, David Jeffries, showed tremendous courage by entering the crumbling crypt of a fifteenth-century church that stands in ruins on the outskirts of the town, to rescue the missing guide dog, Bella. She was found alive and well after almost two weeks, after having been terrified by fireworks on November 5th. After what ended one of the biggest searches of its kind, David told our reporter, Mike Bretton, how he found the much-loved black Labrador. He said, "With the help of Mr Tom Sinclair and some school friends, I managed to clear debris from a trapdoor. This revealed steps leading down into the crypt of the old church ruin. Bella had remained trapped there for almost two weeks without food or water."

In spite of the steps leading down into the crypt being

in a very dangerous condition, David, with no thought to his own safety, climbed down into the crypt to rescue Bella, the beloved companion and guide dog of Mr Tom Sinclair.

When asked about his ordeal, the shy hero stated, "I didn't really think about the danger, I just knew I had to get Bella out safely."

Basher took a deliberately deep breath before going on.

After a comfortable night at home with her owner, Bella showed little sign of her ordeal. A delighted Mr Sinclair said, "I can't tell you what it means to have Bella back home with me." He went on to praise the courage of David and his friends, and also paid tribute to Madame Francesca, the Claire....?'

Basher struggled with the word.

"Clairvoyant!" exclaimed Melanie, irritated that Basher was unable to read the word.

"All right!" said an indignant Basher. "I can read!" Then he continued reading the front page of the newspaper.

'....Madame Francesca, the clairvoyant. "Without her help," added Mr Sinclair gratefully, "we might never have found Bella at all. It's a miracle she was still alive." Preparations are under way to give this famous guide dog a Welcome Home party that is planned to be held at the Grand Hotel on Saturday next at 2.30 pm. It is hoped that Sir Richard Pringle, President of the Guide Dogs for the Blind Association, will be there. There will also be a presentation of the reward money of one hundred pounds that Mr Sinclair promised to pay anyone who found Bella. Also many other dignitaries will be present for this happy occasion.'

Melanie was the first to comment after Basher finished. "So!" she smiled, "David's a hero now!" Basher noticed the look of admiration on Melanie's pretty face.

"Huh!" he scoffed, "Anyone can be a hero." He shrugged

his shoulders as he folded the newspaper. "You just have to be in the right place at the right time.... that's all." Melanie looked at Basher knowingly.

"I do believe you're jealous, Basher." Little Tim giggled at his friend's embarrassment.

"You must be joking!" retorted Basher angrily, blushing bright pink at the same time. Little Tim cuffed him playfully.

"I bet you are!" he teased. Basher refused to say any more on the subject and suggested they hurry or they would miss their buses.

Melanie shivered against the chill of the late afternoon as she wrapped her school scarf around her neck and tossed it over her shoulder. "Are you going on Saturday?" she asked Basher, meaning Little Tim too.

"You bet we are," said a determined Basher, "We're not going to miss out on all the fun." Little Tim nodded agreement, then they each made their way to their respective buses.

* * * * *

David's ankle had swollen considerably overnight, so much so his mother took him to the doctor who, fortunately, was able to confirm that it was no more than a bad sprain. He strapped up David's ankle and sent him away with hearty congratulations on his heroic deed. News spread quickly, thought David as he hobbled out of the doctor's surgery.

Marion Jeffries had telephoned Mr Mason as soon as she had the good news to advise that they were all safely home. Her feelings of anxiety had been quickly replaced with feelings of pride and excitement. She couldn't wait to tell everyone the good news. She had suggested the idea of a 'welcome home' party to the PE teacher, who thought it a wonderful idea. He suggested they use the school hall. However, Marion had more grand ideas for what was, after all, a very special occasion for a famous guide dog.

Marion spent the whole day organising and arranging

for the various guests to attend. She was a little concerned about the cost of the Grand Hotel, that was until the manager said in view of the occasion there would be no charge for the hire.... just for the catering. Marion knew she could rely on the generous support of many of the parents and teachers to contribute to the cost. She finally went to bed exhausted but happy.

News of Bella's rescue was carried by all TV networks and radio stations, both locally and nationally the following day. Magazines and periodicals tried to out-do each other for exclusive interviews. Tom found it all quite staggering that so many people were interested. In the days that followed, there were dozens of telegrams and cards congratulating Tom and Bella.

And the telephone calls! They were non-stop. Friends, neighbours and complete strangers were ringing his home until his head was dizzy. For the next two days Tom and Bella's lives were a whirlwind of excitement. And there was more to come......

One-thirty on Saturday afternoon found Marion Jeffries and Mr Mason, with David, Claire and Rosie arriving at the entrance to the Grand Hotel, looking resplendent in their party gear. They were unconcerned about the grey day, for they knew that this was one day that the sun would shine from within. As they were ushered into the Banqueting Room it was a sight to behold. The blue and white sculptured walls and ceiling, royal blue velvet curtains and the magnificent glass chandeliers made a wonderful backcloth for the ornate gilded blue velvet upholstered chairs set around the dance floor. Rosie and Claire looked at each other in amazement.

At one end of the room a sumptuous buffet had been set out and at the other end there was a raised dais on which there was a solitary microphone. Close by was a table covered in a white cloth upon which several ice-buckets were holding bottles of champagne; donated by a local well-wisher. On the other side of the dais was an electronic organ on which the musician was practising in readiness for the occasion.

To complete the picture, there was a banner of red silk draped over the dais with the words in large white print WELCOME HOME BELLA. Alongside the dais Claire and Rosie spotted a large red satin cushion, with gold tassels at each corner, laid in readiness for Bella.

"Look at that!" said Claire in sheer wonderment. The others looked on almost speechless.

Mr Mason expressed his appreciation of the way the management at the Grand Hotel had gone to so much trouble to make the occasion very special. His eyes followed the deep red carpet that ran the full length of the room from the door to the dais. "Bella certainly has an effect on people," he said with pride - pride at being privileged to know Tom and his lovable guide dog, Bella. Marion found herself echoing his praise. David, still limping slightly, was quietly proud of the honour of being at such an occasion, although he felt a little nervous about the whole thing.

By two o'clock the Mayor of Barrington had arrived, also Sir Richard Pringle. Other dignitaries arrived, as did parents and the schoolchildren. Then Madame Francesca whom Marion greeted and introduced to Mr Mason. More and more guests arrived, and newspaper reporters and TV crews were also in evidence. Jimmy now joined David and the others, and waved to Basher and Melanie who were with their parents.

Mr Mason had arranged for a taxi to collect Tom and Bella from their home at ten minutes past two. This would give all the guests time to arrive ahead of them, so that Bella could make her grand entrance. There was a hum of excitement around the Banqueting Room as the guests waited for Tom and Bella to arrive. Mr Mason glanced at his watch, estimating that Tom and Bella should be arriving at any minute.

Mr Mason turned to Marion, saying, "Will you please excuse me for a moment?" looking anxiously in the direction of the main doors, "I have a feeling Tom and Bella have arrived." At that very moment the large doors swung open, and.... there stood Bella for all to see.... alive and well, beside Tom. A resounding cheer went up which must surely have been heard throughout the whole hotel. Bella was getting the star treatment and responded as she always did to such a show of love and devotion, her happy tail was waving frantically in the air. Mr Mason made his way to Tom's side and briefed him quickly about the walk straight ahead on the red carpet that led to the dais.

Tom looked very smart indeed in his grey pin-striped suit, white shirt and plum coloured striped tie. At first he looked slightly dazed but then a smile, which spoke volumes, spread across his cleanly shaven face as he and Bella began the walk down the red carpet towards the dais. Bella's black coat was shining beautifully and, although she had lost a little weight, she was as she had always been, a real 'star'.

The organist struck a chord and everyone began singing 'Welcome Home' as Tom and Bella walked slowly the full length of the room. It was a moment that took Tom back to that wonderful day in Barrington. He felt the same tingle up his spine, and the same emotions that he felt then; there were no words to describe how he felt. He could hear the cameras clicking on either side of him. He stopped when he felt Mr Mason's arm, just in front of the dais where, once the singing had finished, everyone cheered and clapped.

Mr Mason introduced Tom to the Mayor of Barrington once again, and to Sir Richard Pringle, the Association's president. As the cheering subsided, the Mayor addressed everyone present; he estimated there were well over three hundred people in the room.

"Ladies and gentlemen," he called, "Could we have three cheers for Bella, to welcome her home. Hip! Hip!...." Then the whole room responded with "HOORAY!" followed by more hand-clapping.

The Mayor and Sir Richard shook hands with Tom and

led Bella to her red satin cushion. Explaining to Tom in a low voice as he guided him to a chair beside the cushion, "Come on, Bella," said the Mayor so all could hear, "we have a very special seat for you." Bella, looking every bit a 'star', sat on her red satin cushion. She looked resplendent, her black fur shining against the red of the cushion, a stark contrast to the misery she had had to endure in the ruins of the old church. The press were having a field day, their cameras clicking away for a full two minutes before the Mayor could continue with his speech.

"Thank you!" he said in a loud voice, endeavouring to gain everyone's attention. At last he was able to continue, "It goes without saying how delighted we all are to see Bella back home, safe and well." He sighed as he explained, "We all know what a worrying time these last two weeks have been, especially for Tom." He looked at Tom, who nodded as he sat with his head bowed, listening to the Mayor's every word. "But!" said the Mayor, with a wave of his hand, "Today is a day for celebration, so I'm not going to waste it with long speeches." There were a few cheers from some of the dignitaries around the room. The Mayor waved, and then turned to Sir Richard, "Sir Richard, perhaps you would like to say a few words."

Sir Richard Pringle exchanged places with the Mayor and stood in front of the microphone as he said, "Yes, I would, Mr Mayor. Thank you!"

He looked around the room as he said, "This is indeed a very happy day for us all." Letting his eyes rest on Bella on her cushion, he added, "What a marvellous sight it is to see Bella here, safe and well, and none the worse for her ordeal. We are all well aware of the tremendous amount of charity work Tom and Bella have done for the Association in the past. I am sure," he said, looking at Tom, "with Bella back at Tom's side, they can look forward to an even brighter future together." This comment drew a huge round of applause from the guests. The Mayor stepped up to the microphone at this juncture, saying light-heartedly, "I doubt if there's anyone happier than Tom right now.... with the exception of Bella, of course." Everyone laughed in agreement.

The Mayor invited Tom to say a few words before the reward money was presented. There was a hush all around the room as Tom stood in front of the microphone and looked into the void in front of him. He wrung his hands nervously, and said, "Well! This must be the happiest day of my life," he spoke slowly and with deep emotion. "I can't begin to tell you what it means to have Bella safely back with me once more. Believe me, the past couple of weeks have been Hell," he raised both his hands in an open gesture, "But... this is Heaven!" through the cheering that followed, he shouted, "And I thank God!" He had to wait for a full minute before he could continue.

"I would also like to thank a few young friends, because without their help.... this celebration might not have been possible. As you all know...." he said, reaching for an envelope from his inside jacket pocket, "I offered one hundred pounds to anyone who could find Bella for me. Well, I think you will all agree that while Claire, Jimmy and Rosie were instrumental in securing Bella's safe return, the real hero of the day has to be..," he sensed the tension in the room before he confirmed, "David.... David Jeffries!" Tom clapped his hands heartily, along with everyone else. David felt a blush of embarrassment but he found comfort in Rosie's smile as Tom continued. "David showed tremendous courage by risking his own life in order to save Bella. I can never thank him enough, and I am sure you will all agree that the reward money should go to David."

The loud round of applause told Tom all he needed to know. He asked if David would make his way to the microphone to receive his reward. Rosie gave him a loving wink, as he left the group to go up to the dais. As he reached the dais Tom put out a hand and David took it, and joined Tom at the microphone. "David!" said the delighted blind man, "You don't know how happy I am to give you this reward money." Bella upon seeing David left the red cushion and was by his side, wagging her happy tail, as if to say, "no one could be more delighted than I am."

David felt himself blush as Tom once again praised his courage before presenting him with the cheque. "It gives me great pleasure indeed to present you with this cheque for one hundred pounds." David accepted the cheque graciously, mentioning that some of the praise should go to his friends and, of course, to Madame Francesca, the clairvoyant. Tom agreed and called out for her to take a bow. She was sitting further down the room and Tom asked everyone to give her a big round of applause, and as she sat down Madame Francesca blew a kiss to Bella.

As David thanked Tom and was about to leave the dais Tom suggested he stayed where he was for the moment. Tom then asked if Rosie, Claire and Jimmy would join them. He heard their footsteps approach the dais and held out his hand which Rosie shook.

"Now!" he said, looking in the direction of the trio, "Rosie, Claire and Jimmy have also been instrumental in the search and rescue of Bella, so I couldn't possibly let this occasion go by without thanking them in some small way." There was muted laughter coming from around the room and Tom sensed Bella was up to something. "Not now Bella!" Jimmy whispered, trying hard to control his laughter from the tickling. Bella, thinking they had come to play, was making her usual attempt to search Jimmy's pocket for the tennis ball he always carried on the playing field.

Tom said lovingly, "Here, Bella!" and she was immediately by his side. He then took out three more envelopes from his inside jacket pocket. He then asked Bella to hand the first envelope to Rosie, the second to Claire and the third to Jimmy. There was another round of applause for the children and especially for the clever guide dog, Bella; Bella loved it, she sat with her paw in the air asking for more. Tom then asked David if he would put Bella back on the cushion for him, which he did.

Meanwhile, Rosie was opening the envelope given to her, and Claire and Jimmy followed suit. "Fifty pounds!" exclaimed a flabbergasted Rosie. "Me too," said a delighted Claire.

"And I've got fifty pounds, too," said Jimmy in his high-pitched excited voice. "But Tom," he said, forgetting his nerves at being up on the dais in front of so many people, "You've already paid out one hundred pounds reward money.... I can't possibly take this from you."

Tom smiled, "Let's just say, it's a little something from Bella. Oh, and don't worry Jimmy," Tom assured him, "I had a little money put by for a rainy day but now.... ?" he looked in the direction of Bella on her cushion, "Now I have enough sunshine to last me a lifetime."

Rosie could see that there was no way she could refuse the money, "Thank you, Tom," she smiled. "You are very generous." Claire thanked him and kissed him affectionately on the cheek, while Jimmy just stood speechless.

Jimmy looked at the cheque for fifty pounds and said, "Just for once, Tom, I'm lost for words." This caused a few ripples of laughter from all those who knew the jovial, vociferous, Jimmy Lucas.

"Well now," said Tom humourously, "that makes quite a change for you Jimmy." The others laughed, but none more than Jimmy himself. Just at that moment Mr Mason came hurrying up to the dais where the Mayor and Sir Richard were looking on in amusement.

"I wonder if I could interrupt you for a moment," he said apologetically. "I don't want to hold things up but I thought everyone would like to know I am putting David's name forward for the National Award for Bravery." David looked at his friends with astonished eyes, as applause drowned Mr Mason's words.

"Why that's champion!" said a delighted Tom, "I'm sure he'll get it too."

Tom was aware now that he really should speed things up if they were to get on with the celebrations. He concluded by thanking all the many people who had helped in the search for Bella, and for all the kindness that had been shown to him personally. Mr Mason, who was still on the dais requested that he might say one more thing before the celebrations got under way. The Mayor nodded his agreement.

"Tom," he said, "I am delighted to be able to present to you.... on behalf of the children...." He reached for an envelope from his pocket. As he did so a frown crossed Tom's face, ".... a cheque for eight hundred and ninety-four pounds and twenty-eight pence, to give to the charity nearest to your heart." There were more than a few gasps from around those assembled as Mr Mason handed Tom the cheque.

Tom was staggered by such generosity, "That's absolutely marvellous.... but how....?"

Mr Mason explained, "Unknown to you, Tom, David and his friends were determined that you should have another guide dog, in the event that Bella wasn't found. They organised a School Disco and an Autumn Fayre which, I might add, were tremendously successful." At the sound of her name, Bella left her cushion and joined Mr Mason and Tom at the microphone, wagging her happy tail once more. Mr Mason smiled and patted her affectionately. "I'm delighted that we didn't need to use the money, but I must say all the children worked like Trojans." He looked out across the Banqueting Room. "Perhaps, at this point, I could just say a big thank you to Basher, Melanie and Tim McCreadie, as well as David and his friends - just to mention a few - and to all the many parents who were a tremendous help. Thank you all!"

Tom held the envelope close to his heart and sighed softly, "Now it's my turn to say 'I don't know what to say', and I really don't." He smiled, "Now I know how young Jimmy felt." All eyes were on Jimmy for a moment. "What I do know," said Tom, "is that such kindness warms my heart.

It really does." Tom then looked in the direction of Sir Richard Pringle and asked him if he would be so kind as to accept the cheque on behalf of the Guide Dogs for the Blind Association. Tom then stooped to Bella and gave her the envelope, "There Bella, you will have great pleasure in presenting this cheque to Sir Richard."

Everyone smiled as Bella took the envelope with the cheque in it to Sir Richard as he extended his hand to receive it. He patted Bella as everyone clapped and cheered once more.

Sir Richard felt that he could not let this moment go without adding his personal thank you. He addressed everyone in the room and smiled, "May I just say, as always, the Association is deeply indebted to the public for their generous support in helping to raise funds, in order that we may provide guide dogs for the blind. However," here there was a slight hint of emotion in his voice, "when a group of children goes to all this trouble, and works so hard in order to raise funds.... then we are deeply moved." He smiled at Bella, "It would seem that the love that Bella generates, knows no bounds." All eyes were on Bella now, who was seated back on the red satin cushion, her large ebony eyes darting back and forth; she wasn't going to miss a trick. Applause rang out again and Bella loved it.

Marion Jeffries made her way to the dais, while the applause continued, and had a quick word with Sir Richard. He nodded as the applause died down. Marion could be heard to say in a slightly trembling voice, "Sir Richard, knowing that the children had set their hearts on a target of one thousand pounds, we at the Women's Institute decided to raise a few funds of our own. And...." she smiled, "I'm delighted to be able to give you a cheque for one hundred and five pounds, and seventy-two pence, making a total of one thousand pounds." She rushed the last of her words and finished quite out of breath.

David and Claire were unaware of this effort by their mother and her friends at the local WI. As their mother

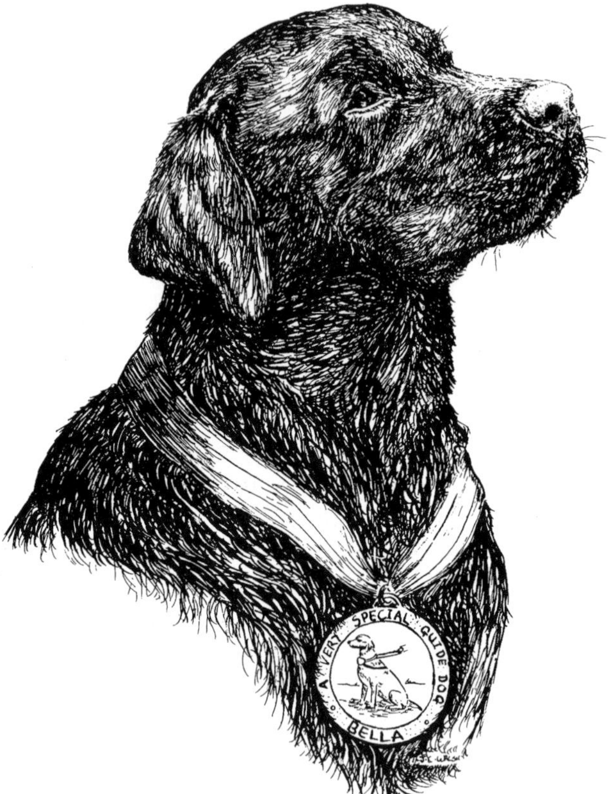
A VERY SPECIAL GUIDE DOG
BELLA

returned to their group, David and Claire gave her a big hug and kissed her cheek. Sir Richard then spoke once more.

"Thank you very much indeed.... this is tremendous." He shook his head, again touched by such generosity. Sir Richard had one more task to perform before the party progressed. He addressed the guests once more, "Now, it's Bella's turn," he said, taking a large black box from his pocket. There were gasps from around the room as he opened it to reveal a large gold coloured medal, attached to a red satin ribbon. He called Bella to him and she sat at his feet, waiting. Tom had a quizzical look on his face as he listened to the proceedings. Then he felt a glow in his heart.... a glow of pride, as Sir Richard continued.

"We don't usually give medals to guide dogs. However," he stressed, "in Bella's case we have made an exception and decided to award her the VSGD." He explained, "A VERY SPECIAL GUIDE DOG!" Amid rapturous applause Sir Richard placed the ribbon over Bella's head until the gold coloured medal hung proudly around the guide dog's neck. Tom was moved beyond words as he stood in the midst of all the cheering; he felt so proud of his beloved Bella.

The Mayor came forward to the microphone. "Congratulations, Bella!" he said, taking the black Labrador's paw and shaking it gently. "What a marvellous day this is turning out to be." He looked at the waiter who was about to pop the champagne corks ready for the toast. "I think this calls for a champagne toast to Bella." There were more cheers as the waiters began to pour the champagne and pass the glasses around to the guests. The staff had gone to the trouble of making a non-alcoholic drink for the children consisting of Kiwi fruits, lemonade and crushed lemon ice.

As soon as the Mayor was sure everyone had a glass in their hand, he addressed them once again. "I would like to propose a toast," he said looking at Bella, who, having seen the photographers, poised, ready to take her picture, she was preening ready, ever the 'star'. "To one of the bravest, lovable guide dogs I've ever known." There was a resounding "Hear! Hear!" from around the room. "And so," the Mayor concluded, raising his glass high in the air, "TO BELLA!" he toasted. There was a resounding reply, "TO BELLA!"

Once the photographers had finished taking their pictures, the Mayor requested music and for everyone to start enjoying themselves. The Mayor saw to it that Tom had a place of honour in the Banqueting Room with Bella on her red satin cushion beside him, where people could make a fuss of her. Within minutes a hail of hands and hearty congratulations besieged Tom and Bella.

There was still a small crowd of people around them when Tom felt a slight tap on his shoulder from behind. He smiled knowingly as a voice said, "Hello! Mr Sinclair. Remember me?"

Tom immediately recognised her voice and proffered his hand. "Why, it's Mrs Boardman, Bella's puppy-walker. This is a surprise," he said, shaking her hand vigorously. "How are you?" Phyllis Boardman moved nearer to the front of Tom as some of the well-wishers dispersed.

"I'm very well, thank you." She gave Bella a big hug. "Oh Bella, do you remember me?" She was afraid Bella would have long forgotten her puppy-walking days, but the excited guide dog's muted squeals of delight, accompanied by a happy tail waving in all directions, told her that Bella hadn't forgotten her.

Tom and Phyllis had lots to talk about, but before going back to her seat, she made Tom promise that she could have a dance with him before the day was through. As she made her way back across the room the organist played 'Welcome Home' again and just about everybody got up to dance.

Marion Jeffries danced with Mr Mason, David happily danced with Rosie; he closed his eyes as his cheek brushed hers. What a brilliant day it had been. He looked into Rosie's eyes with that thought running over and over in his mind. Rosie smiled lovingly at David, who hugged her tightly. It was a hug that said - I love you.

Jimmy had plucked up courage and asked Claire to dance, but they seemed to be having some difficulty agreeing on the same steps. After a minute or two Claire stopped and stood still on the dance floor. She put both hands on her hips and sighed at her partner, "Have you got two left feet, Jimmy Lucas?"

"No!" Jimmy answered cheekily, "have you?" and he laughed out loud at his own joke.

However, Claire was not amused, "You never change, do you?" she said huffily. She took hold of the jovial Jimmy once more saying, "Come on!" She sounded impatient now, "Just follow my feet.... Ouch!" Jimmy said he was sorry but he still had a broad grin on his face. Claire just rolled her eyes and sighed again.

David and Rosie, having heard them, smiled knowingly. They decided that Jimmy and Claire really did like each other but it was just that some people showed their emotions in a different way.

The dancing continued for a while and with most people up on the dance floor, Tom actually found himself alone with Bella for a few minutes. He felt exhausted from all the excitement and talking. Bella too had found it rather hectic. She sat beside Tom, leaning her weary head on his knee. Now and again her nose would twitch at the smell of food coming from the buffet, tantalising her senses. She was, of course, unaware that a special meal had been prepared for her by the hotel staff. It was being held back until it coincided with the usual time for her feed. This way her feeding habits would not be disturbed, so important for a working guide dog, expected to keep to a strict toilet routine.

This welcome respite from the endless stream of visitors gave Tom time to reflect on all that had happened. He gently stroked Bella as he recalled what had happened and the wonder of it all. As he sat with the sound of 'Welcome Home' - which meant so much to him - running through his mind, he knew without a doubt that this was the happiest time of his life.

Tom continued to stroke Bella as he thought about all the generosity of so many people and most of all the children, raising all that money in so short a time. Those wonderful young people, they could teach us all so much he thought with incredulity. The champagne donated by a well-wisher and the Grand Hotel donating the room free of charge, complete with organist and chef for the day. There was David's award for bravery; meeting Bella's puppy-walker again after all this time and, as if that wasn't enough, there was Bella's award for 'A Very Special Guide Dog'.

Tom's fingers probed around Bella's neck for the medal, down the red satin ribbon, until he found it. His fingers' sensitive touch told him there was an embossed guide dog, complete with harness, and the name 'Bella' underneath. He felt around the outer circle of it, to make out the words - A Very Special Guide Dog. He leaned a little closer to Bella and whispered, "I'm so proud of you, Bella." She replied with a little squeal of delight and a quick swish of her happy tail. If only she could have talked she would have also said, "This is the happiest day of my life."

As Tom listened to all the happiness and laughter, music and dancing, he cherished a few more minutes of quietness. He knew he would soon be asked to join the Mayor and Sir Richard at the VIP's table, and so he wanted to savour this moment. He thought about the conversation he had had with Phyllis Boardman and her kind letter. It reminded Tom of when he first teamed up with Bella.

Since that day Bella had given him so much. He thought wistfully about all the important people she had met, stars and Royalty too; he thought about the fifty mile walk to celebrate the Association's Golden Jubilee; he recalled the way Bella had saved his life from a vicious attack in the park; about the day she went missing and the day she was found; and today, the very special guide dog award; the pride, the love and the loyalty. Yes, he thought mistily, Bella had given him so very much.

Bella looked at her blind owner with her great big ebony eyes and lovingly rested her chin on his lap. Nothing could part them now, thought Tom, but he was painfully aware of the fact that a guide dog's average working life is only ten years at the most. He was sure there would be other dogs in his life. But, as he sat stroking the silky black fur on the ears of his guide dog, he knew there would never be another Bella....... never.

THE END